Learning Subsequential Transducers. A Categorical Approach

Riccardo Stabile

GRIN

Bibliographic information published by the German National Library:

The German National Library lists this publication in the National Bibliography; detailed bibliographic data are available on the Internet at http://dnb.dnb.de.

ISBN: 9783389015650
This book is also available as an ebook.

Print and binding: Books on Demand GmbH, Norderstedt, Germany
Printed on acid-free paper from responsible sources.

FACOLTÀ DI SCIENZE E TECNOLOGIE
Corso di Laurea Magistrale in Matematica

MASTER THESIS

Learning subsequential transducers: a categorical approach

Author:
Riccardo Stabile

Academic Year 2022-2023

If people do not believe that mathematics is simple,
it is only because they do not realize how complicated life is.

John Von Neumann, quoted by Franz Leopold Alt in
Archaeology of Computers - Reminiscences, 1945-1947,
1972

Contents

Abstract

In this thesis, an algorithm for learning subsequential transducers is presented from two different perspectives: as an extension of Angluin's algorithm for learning deterministic finite automata and as an instantiation of the original and more generic categorical FunL*-algorithm valid for a larger class of automata. The adopted categorical approach considers automata as functors from a category representing words to a certain output category. Some sufficient properties for yielding the existence of minimal automata are presented, together with some additional hypotheses relative to termination to ensure the correctness of the generic algorithm.

Introduction

It is not uncommon to understand facts, processes and results better by looking at them from above: learning is not an exception.

Learning is a crucial area in computer science, especially in artificial intelligence: knowing how to deal with communication, mistakes and experience plays an essential role to progress in learning.

But even more important is learning what makes communication possible: a language.

A language can be initially thought as a subset of a set of words over an alphabet, always supposed to be finite.

The relation between languages and automata has become clearer and clearer in the last decades, since Noam Chomsky gave a mathematical model of a grammar in the second half of the last century.

A deterministic finite automaton accepts a language, called regular, and for every regular language there exists a deterministic finite automaton being minimal, i.e. with a minimal number of states, that accepts it.

An analogous thing happens for subsequential transducers, which are automata more complex than deterministic finite automata: in this case, some partial functions, called subsequential, from a set of words to another over possibly different alphabets are accepted; a subsequential transducer accepts a particular subsequential function and for every subsequential function there exists a minimal subsequential transducer accepting it.

This is the reason why learning regular languages and subsequential functions may be pursued by learning the minimal automata accepting them.

The L^*-algorithm of Angluin is certainly the most famous algorithm for learning deterministic finite automata; its goal is to learn the minimal automaton accepting a regular language $\mathcal{L}$ by means of the interactions between two key figures: a learner and a teacher.

Its indubitable strength consists not only in being extremely efficient and understandable, but also in catching the role played by the most important actors of the learning process.

Angluin's algorithm has turned out to be so robust that it has been extended to several other forms of automata, such as nominal automata [16], omega automata [3], non-deterministic automata [5], alternating automata [2] and symbolic automata [12].

To highlight what may be the utility of extending Angluin's algorithm to subsequential transducers, it may be remarked that integer division, integer multiplication and many classical other functions are subsequential, as well as decoding and substituting patterns (see [6, 18]).

Showing how to extend Angluin's algorithm to subsequential transducers is what the first part of this thesis is devoted to; notice that, although developed independently, the presented f^*-algorithm is very similar to the one already investigated by Vilar in [22].

What about pushing this process even further? What about trying to recognize the deeper patterns underlying the interactions between the learner and the teacher?

Mathematics provides an extremely powerful tool to do that: category theory.

It is not the first time that results of automata learning have been interpreted from a categorical perspective: in recent years, several coalgebraic approaches have been proposed, starting with the perspective of [15] and continuing with the CALF framework of van Heerdt et al. [21]; a duality theoretic perspective was also presented in [4]; another generic algorithm was proposed in [20].

Nevertheless, none of these frameworks cover the learning algorithm for subsequential transducers.

Starting from the working framework developed in [10, 11], where automata are considered as functors from a fixed three-object category to an output category $\mathcal{C}$, an abstract categorical version of Angluin's L^*-algorithm is provided in the second part of this thesis: it can be instantiated with a large class of automata by varying the output category, deterministic finite automata and subsequential transducers included.

The categorical presentation of this new algorithm, called FunL*-algorithm, is strongly based on the article [9] written by the author together with Professors Thomas Colcombet and Daniela Petrişan during a five-month study period at Université de Paris in 2020.

Not only this presentation of the L^*-algorithm covers more instances of learning algorithms than prior descriptions via categories of classical word automata, but also highlights the strong relationship between learning and minimizing automata: indeed, each elementary step of the algorithm involves performing a minimization-like computation.

The two parts of the thesis are composed as follows.

Part I adopts the lens of query learning: the original Angluin's algorithm for deterministic finite automata is recalled in Chapter 1 and its extension to subsequential transducers is described in Chapter 2.

Part II adopts the lens of category theory: the general working framework of the algorithm together with sufficient conditions to minimize automata are presented in Chapter 3; the FunL*-algorithm and other mild conditions to make it work are presented in Chapter 4; finally, in Chapter 5 the FunL*-algorithm is instantiated to learn subsequential transducers, while the simpler case of deterministic finite automata is analysed throughout the two previous chapters, in order to familiarize the reader with minimizing automata and running the FunL*-algorithm.

Remarkably, the conditions required in Angluin's original L^*-algorithm and in its extended version for subsequential transducers naturally arise as the generic FunL*-algorithm is instantiated with the proper output categories.

Part I

Learning automata from queries and counterexamples

Learning starts with failure,
the first failure is the beginning of education.

John Richard Hersey,
The Child Buyer,
1960

Chapter 1

Angluin's learning algorithm

In this chapter, Angluin's original L^*-algorithm for learning deterministic finite automata is presented.

The main reference is her article published in 1987, [1].

Thanks to this algorithm, an unknown regular language, the *target language*, may be learnt, by eventually giving the minimal automaton accepting it.

In order to do that, who puts in place the algorithm, the learner, can ask to who knows the language, the teacher, two kinds of queries:

- *membership queries*, in which the learner selects a word and the teacher says if it belong to the language or not;

- *equivalence queries*, in which the learner selects an hypothesis DFA and asks the teacher if the language it accepts is the target language, getting a counterexample in case of negative answer.

It is assumed that the learner knows the alphabet over which the target language is.

A key property of the L^*-algorithm is that it terminates in time polynomial in the size of the minimal deterministic automaton for the language and of the longest given counterexample.

After recalling the notion of deterministic finite automaton and what it means for it to be minimal, it will be described how to build up hypothesis deterministic finite automata according to what the learner has already discovered during the learning process.

Then, the algorithm will be presented, together with a short example of running in Section 1.6.

1.1 Deterministic finite automata

Let's start with some simple definitions.

Definition 1.1.1. An *alphabet* A is a finite non-empty set, whose elements are said to be *letters*.

Definition 1.1.2. A *word* on an alphabet A is a finite concatenation of letters in A, possibly repeated; the *empty word* ε, i.e. the word containing no letters, and all the letters in A are words too.

Definition 1.1.3. Let A be an alphabet. A^* is the *set of words on* A.

Definition 1.1.4. A *language* $\mathcal{L}$ over an alphabet A is a subset $\mathcal{L} \subseteq A^*$.

It is now possible to define what deterministic finite automata are, together with the language they accept.

Definition 1.1.5. A *deterministic finite automaton*, or *DFA*, is a tuple

$$(Q, A, q_0, F, (\delta_a)_{a \in A})$$

where:

- Q is a finite set of states;
- A is an alphabet;
- $q_0 \in Q$ is the initial state;
- $F \subseteq Q$ is the set of final states;
- $\delta_a : Q \to Q$ is the transition function for all $a \in A$.

Definition 1.1.6. Given a word $e = a_1 \ldots a_n$, $a_i \in A$, a DFA *accepts* it if $\delta_{a_n} \circ \ldots \circ \delta_{a_1}(q_0) \in F$; the language accepted by the automaton is the subset of A^* whose elements are accepted.

A regular language is defined consequently.

Definition 1.1.7. A language $\mathcal{L} \subseteq A^*$ is said to be *regular* if there exists a DFA accepting it.

For the sake of completeness, it may be pointed out that there exist several equivalent characterizations of regular languages which do not make use of DFA.
This thesis does not focus on such aspects; the interested reader may refer for instance to the classical [13, 14] for further details.

Example 1.1.8. Let's consider the following DFA, called *DFAex*.

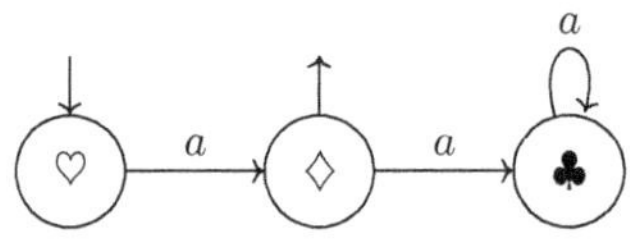

Figure 1.1.9. The deterministic finite automaton DFAex.

The diagram should be interpreted as follows:

- the set of states is $\{\heartsuit, \diamondsuit, \clubsuit\}$;
- the alphabet is $\{a\}$;
- $\heartsuit$ is the initial state and $\{\diamondsuit\}$ is the set of final states;
- the transition map for a maps a state to the one its outgoing arrow labelled a goes to.

What is the language $\mathcal{L} \subseteq \{a\}^*$ accepted by DFAex?

Let's adopt the notation $x^n := xx \ldots x$, with x repeated n times and being the empty word if $n = 0$: it is therefore clear that $\{a\}^* = \{a^i | i \in \mathbb{N}\}$.

For $i = 0$, one gets ε being rejected, because $\heartsuit$ is not a final state.

For $i = 1$, one gets a being accepted, because $\diamondsuit$ is a final state.

For a greater value of i, one always has that $\delta_a \circ \ldots \circ \delta_a(\heartsuit) = \clubsuit$, which is not a final state, so a^i is rejected.

It turns out that the accepted language is composed by the only word a.

1.2 Minimal deterministic finite automata

Definition 1.2.1. A DFA accepting a regular language $\mathcal{L}$ is said to be *minimal* if there does not exist a DFA accepting $\mathcal{L}$ with fewer states.

For every regular language $\mathcal{L}$, the minimal DFA accepting $\mathcal{L}$ exists and is unique up to renaming of states.

The following description of the minimal DFA accepting a regular language is based on the proof of the Myhill-Nerode Theorem.

All the proofs can be found in [13, 14].

Definition 1.2.2. Let $\mathcal{L}$ be a language over A and let T be a subset of A^*.

The *T-syntactic equivalence relation over $\mathcal{L}$* is defined as follows, for all $x, y \in A^*$:

$$x \sim_T y \text{ if and only if } \forall t \in T (xt \in \mathcal{L} \Leftrightarrow yt \in \mathcal{L}).$$

Notice that the dependence on T may not be pointed out if $T = A^*$.

Theorem 1.2.3 (Myhill-Nerode Theorem)**.** *Let $\mathcal{L}$ be a language.*

$\mathcal{L}$ is regular if and only if the syntactic equivalence relation over $\mathcal{L}$ has finite index; assuming regularity, such an index equals the number of states of the minimal automaton accepting $\mathcal{L}$.

As a matter of notation, let $Q/{\sim_T}$ denote the set Q quotiented by the T-syntactic equivalence relation over $\mathcal{L}$, Q and T being two subsets of A^*:

$$Q/{\sim_T} = \{[u]_T : u \in Q\}.$$

If $Q = T = A^*$, the following notation is adopted for the syntactic equivalence relation over $\mathcal{L}$:

$$A^*/{\sim} = \{[u] : u \in A^*\}.$$

Proposition 1.2.4. *Up to renaming of states, the minimal deterministic finite automaton accepting a regular language $\mathcal{L}$ is the tuple*

$$(Q_{min}, A, q_0, F, (\delta_a)_{a\in A})$$

where:

- $Q_{min} = {}^{A^*}/_{\sim}$;
- *A is the alphabet over which $\mathcal{L}$ is;*
- $q_0 = [\varepsilon]$;
- $F = \{[u]\colon u \in \mathcal{L}\}$;
- *for all $a \in A$*

$$\begin{aligned}\delta_a\colon Q_{min} &\to Q_{min}\\ [u] &\mapsto [ua].\end{aligned}$$

Example 1.2.5. Consider the following DFA.

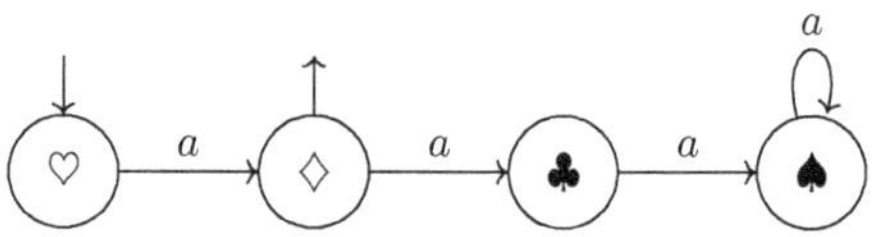

Figure 1.2.6. Another deterministic finite automaton.

This automaton is not minimal: in fact, it accepts the language $\{a\}$, which is also accepted by the three-state automaton DFAex of Figure 1.1.9.

Example 1.2.7. The automaton DFAex represented in Figure 1.1.9, Example 1.1.8, is minimal: to prove it, it suffices to show that $|A^*/{\sim}| \geq 3$, $\sim$ being the syntactic equivalence relation over $\mathcal{L}$, $\mathcal{L} = \{a\}$.

This is true: in fact, $a \nsim \varepsilon$ and $aa \nsim a$, as $aa \notin \mathcal{L} \ni a$; furthermore, $aa \nsim \varepsilon$, as $aaa \notin \mathcal{L} \ni a$; as a result, $[\varepsilon], [a]$ and $[aa]$ are three different equivalence classes in $A^*/{\sim}$.

1.3 Hypothesis deterministic finite automata

In Angluin's L^*-algorithm, the learner keeps in memory a couple (Q, T) of non-empty subsets of A^* such that Q is prefix-closed, i.e. it contains the prefixes of all its elements, while T is suffix-closed, the same for the suffixes; in particular, $\varepsilon \in Q \cap T$.

While Q identifies the set of states of a potential automaton, the elements in T are used to discover if words must be distinguished by the automaton.

Using the membership queries and enlarging properly the two subsets, the learner may make the couple (Q, T) have the following two properties, whose definition makes use of the T-syntactic equivalence relation over $\mathcal{L}$, $\mathcal{L}$ being the target language.

Definition 1.3.1. The couple (Q, T) is said to be *$\mathcal{L}$-complete* if

$$\forall q \in Q \; \forall a \in A \; \exists \widetilde{q} \in Q \colon \widetilde{q} \sim_T qa.$$

Definition 1.3.2. The couple (Q, T) is said to be *$\mathcal{L}$-correct* if

$$\forall q_1, q_2 \in Q \; \forall a \in A \; \forall t \in T \; (q_1 \sim_T q_2 \Rightarrow q_1 \sim_{T \cup \{at\}} q_2).$$

In this way, the learner is able to produce an approximation of $\mathcal{L}$, explicitly an hypothesis deterministic finite automaton associated to such a suitable couple.

Definition 1.3.3. Let (Q, T) be both $\mathcal{L}$-complete and $\mathcal{L}$-correct.
The *hypothesis DFA* associated to the couple (Q, T) is the automaton

$$(Q_{hyp}, A, q_0, F, (\delta_a)_{a \in A})$$

where:

- $Q_{hyp} = Q/\sim_T$;
- A is the alphabet over which $\mathcal{L}$ is;
- $q_0 = [\varepsilon]_T$;
- $F = \{[u]_T \in Q_{hyp} \colon u \in \mathcal{L}\}$;
- for all $a \in A$

$$\begin{aligned} \delta_a \colon Q_{hyp} &\to Q_{hyp} \\ [u]_T &\mapsto [ua]_T. \end{aligned}$$

1.4 Angluin's algorithm for DFA

It is now possible to present Angluin's algorithm for learning deterministic finite automata; for all the proofs related to its correctness and termination, the reader may still refer to [1].

The algorithm takes as input a target regular language $\mathcal{L}$ and outputs the minimal DFA accepting it.

First of all, the couple (Q, T) is initialized to $(\{\varepsilon\}, \{\varepsilon\})$; as long as this couple is not both $\mathcal{L}$-complete and $\mathcal{L}$-correct, further words are added to the subsets Q and T to force these properties to arise, letting the reader build up an hypothesis DFA.

If such an automaton still does not recognize the target language, then a provided counterexample and its prefixes are added to Q.

The L^*-algorithm works by performing these operations until the teacher agrees.

input : minimally adequate teacher of the regular target language $\mathcal{L}$
output: minimal DFA accepting $\mathcal{L}$

$Q := T := \{\varepsilon\}$
repeat
  while *(Q, T) is not both $\mathcal{L}$-complete and $\mathcal{L}$-correct* **do**
    if *(Q, T) is not $\mathcal{L}$-complete* **then**
      add $qa \in QA$ s.t. $\nexists \widetilde{q} \in Q\colon \widetilde{q} \sim_T qa$ to Q
    end
    if *(Q, T) is not $\mathcal{L}$-correct* **then**
      add $at \in AT$ s.t. $\exists q_1, q_2 \in Q\colon q_1 \sim_T q_2 \wedge q_1 \nsim_{T \cup \{at\}} q_2$ to T
    end
  end
  ask an equivalence query for the hypothesis DFA associated to the couple (Q, T)
  if *the answer is no* **then**
    add the provided counterexample and all its prefixes to Q
  end
until *the answer is yes*;
return *the hypothesis DFA associated to the couple (Q, T)*

Algorithm 1.4.1. Angluin's L^*-*algorithm.*

Definition 1.4.2. A word w is said to be a *counterexample* for an hypothesis DFA to accept a language $\mathcal{L}$ if either

- the hypothesis DFA accepts it and $w \notin \mathcal{L}$, or
- the hypothesis DFA does not accept it and $w \in \mathcal{L}$.

In other words, letting $\mathcal{L}'$ be the language accepted by the hypothesis DFA, w belongs to the symmetric difference of $\mathcal{L}$ and $\mathcal{L}'$.

In the algorithm, the following notation is used: given two subsets R and S of A^*, RS denotes the set $\{xy \mid x \in R, y \in S\}$.

1.5 Efficiency of Angluin's algorithm for DFA

For the sake of completeness, let's highlight the efficiency of Angluin's L^*-algorithm in terms of time.

Proposition 1.5.1. *Angluin's L^*-algorithm terminates in time polynomial in the size of the minimal DFA accepting the target language $\mathcal{L}$ and the length of the longest counterexample returned by the teacher.*

1.6 A running DFA example

Let's illustrate the behaviour of the L^*-algorithm when it tries to learn the already met regular language $\{a\} \subseteq \{a\}^*$.

At each step, the algorithm keeps in memory two subsets of words (Q, T), starting with $Q = T = \{\varepsilon\}$.

At the beginning, the algorithm attempts to construct an automaton having as sole state $[\varepsilon]_\varepsilon \in Q/{\sim_T}$, which has to be initial.

The target of the transition labelled a issued from ε has to be determined, but such a transition should go to an element in Q being T-equivalent to $\varepsilon a = a$ and there is no such a word in Q: the pair (Q, T) fails to have the property of $\mathcal{L}$-completeness.

The algorithm tries to fix it by adding the word a to Q.

As a consequence, the new couple $(Q = \{\varepsilon, a\}, T = \{\varepsilon\})$ is stored.

Now, the algorithm tries to construct an automaton of states $Q/{\sim_T} = \{[\varepsilon]_\varepsilon, [a]_\varepsilon\}$: this time, it is possible to construct an a-labelled transition from $\varepsilon \in Q$ to $a \in Q$.

What should be the a-labelled transition issued from a? It should be an element $q \in Q$ being T-equivalent to aa: luckily, there is one, namely ε.

Hence, the learner succeeds in constructing the left hypothesis DFA in Figure 1.6.1; in such a figure, each state is denoted by the representative of the equivalence class it actually is in order to lighten the notation.

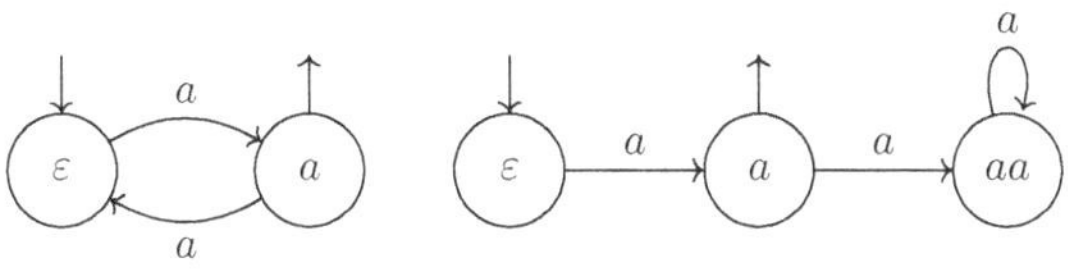

Figure 1.6.1. The two successive hypothesis DFA.

As one can see, the left hypothesis DFA accepts the language $\{a^i : i \text{ is odd}\} \neq \mathcal{L} = \{a\}$, and hence is wrong.

As a consequence, the teacher answers in return a counterexample, say aaa; then, the learner adds all the prefixes of aaa to Q, yielding $Q = \{\varepsilon, a, aa, aaa\}$ and $T = \{\varepsilon\}$.

Now, ε and aa are T-equivalent, but constructing an a-labelled transition from ε would yield a, while constructing one from aa would yield aaa, which is T-equivalent to ε; in other words, $\varepsilon \sim_T aa$, but $\varepsilon \nsim_{T \cup \{a\}} aa$.

Therefore, ε and aa cannot be merged into the same state.

The algorithm compensates it by adding a to T, thus yielding $Q = \{\varepsilon, a, aa, aaa\}$ and $T = \{\varepsilon, a\}$.

Now, the couple (Q, T) is both $\mathcal{L}$-complete and $\mathcal{L}$-correct, and keeping in mind that aa is now T-equivalent to aaa, the right hypothesis deterministic finite automaton in Figure 1.6.1, whose states are $\{[\varepsilon]_{\varepsilon,a}, [a]_{\varepsilon,a}, [aa]_{\varepsilon,a}\}$, can be constructed.

Such an automaton accepts $\{a\}$, so the teacher agrees and the algorithm terminates.

The minimal DFA accepting $\mathcal{L} = \{a\}$ has been produced: as expected, it is exactly, up to renaming of states, the automaton DFAex of Figure 1.1.9, proved to be minimal in Example 1.2.7.

Chapter 2

Learning subsequential transducers

The aim of this chapter is to extend Angluin's L^*-algorithm to subsequential transducers in such a way as to be able to learn an unknown subsequential transduction, called *target transduction*, by eventually giving the minimal subsequential transducer accepting it.

The extended algorithm will be referred to as f^*-algorithm.

To achieve the goal, who puts in place the algorithm, the learner, can ask to who knows the function, the teacher, two kinds of queries:

- *translation queries*, in which the learner selects a word and the teacher returns its image through the target transduction;
- *equivalence queries*, in which the learner selects an hypothesis SST and asks the teacher if the subsequential transduction it accepts is the target transduction, getting a counterexample in case of negative answer.

Translation queries can be thought as the natural generalization of membership queries for the target being a partial function between sets of words, rather than a language.

As in the algorithm for DFA, it will be assumed that the learner knows the underlying alphabets.

After giving the notion of subsequential transducers, the necessary mathematical background will be introduced; then, after showing how to build up hypothesis SST, the f^*-algorithm will be described, together with the proofs of its correctness and termination.

As already pointed out in the introduction, this algorithm, although developed independently, is very similar to the one investigated by Vilar in [22]: the relation between them is highlighted in Remark 2.5.3.

An example of running will be finally illustrated in Section 2.8, so that the reader may deal with the concrete execution of the algorithm.

2.1 Subsequential transducers

Hereafter, B is a fixed output alphabet.

Definition 2.1.1. Let T be a subset of the set of words A^*.
A partial function $g\colon T \rightharpoonup B^*$ is referred to as a *T-transduction*.

Definition 2.1.2. An A^*-transduction $f\colon A^* \rightharpoonup B^*$ is simply referred to as a *transduction*.

To describe what subsequential transducers are and how they work, a double perspective from which T-transductions and partial functions in general can be interpreted should be recalled.

Remark 2.1.3. When dealing with a partial function $h\colon X \rightharpoonup Y$, it may be convenient to express the fact that the image of an element is *undefined* by claiming that it is mapped to a certain symbol not belonging to the involved sets: let it be $\perp$.
For this reason, h may be interpreted as a total function $h\colon X \to Y \cup \{\perp\}$, with the convention of returning $\perp$ for all the elements in X whose image is not defined.
Notice that the employed arrows for partial and total functions are different.

Definition 2.1.4. Let S be a set, $\perp \notin S$. $\overline{S} := S \cup \{\perp\}$ is the *extended* S.

It is now possible to define what a subsequential transducer is.

Definition 2.1.5. A *subsequential transducer*, or *SST*, is a tuple

$$(Q, A, B, q_0, t, u_0, (- \cdot a)_{a \in A}, (- * a)_{a \in A})$$

where:

- Q is a finite set of states;
- A and B are respectively the input and the output alphabets;
- $q_0 \in \overline{Q}$ is the initial state;
- $t\colon Q \rightharpoonup B^*$ is the partial termination function;
- $u_0 \in \overline{B^*}$ is the initialization value, defined if and only if q_0 is;
- $- \cdot a\colon Q \rightharpoonup Q$ is the partial transition function for all $a \in A$;
- $- * a\colon Q \rightharpoonup B^*$ is the partial production function for all $a \in A$, with $q * a$ defined if and only if $q \cdot a$ is, for all $q \in Q$.

Definition 2.1.6. Let S be a subsequential transducer as above.
The transduction *accepted* by S is the partial function $[S]\colon A^* \rightharpoonup B^*$ defined as follows:

$$[S](a_1 a_2 \dots a_n) := u_0(q_0 * a_1)(q_1 * a_2) \dots (q_{n-1} * a_n) t(q_n) \; \forall a_1 a_2 \dots a_n \in A^*,$$

where $q_i := q_{i-1} \cdot a_i$ for all $i \in \{1, 2, \dots, n\}$, the image is defined if and only if $q_0, q_1, \dots, q_n, t(q_n)$ are and the appearing words are just concatenated.

A subsequential transduction is defined consequently.

Definition 2.1.7. A transduction $f\colon A^* \rightharpoonup B^*$ is said to be *subsequential* if there exists a subsequential transducer accepting the transduction f.

Notice that subsequential transductions are also referred to as subsequential functions in the mathematical literature.

As in the DFA case, there exist several equivalent characterizations of subsequential transductions which do not make use of SST.

This thesis does not focus on these aspects; the interested reader may refer to [6, 18] for further details.

Example 2.1.8. The following SST, let it be *SSTex*, is an example of a subsequential transducer operating a pattern substitution.

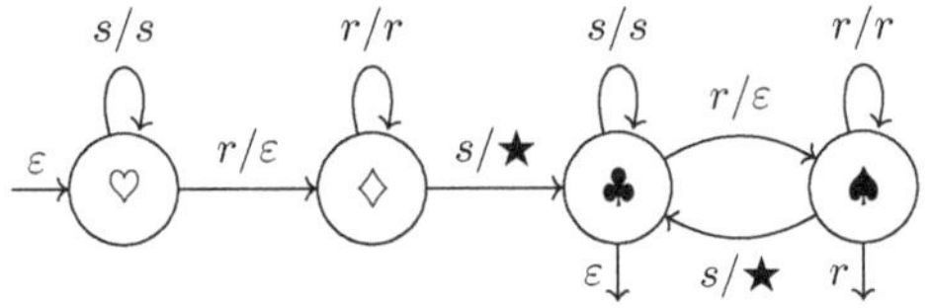

Figure 2.1.9. The subsequential transducer SSTex.

The subsequential transducer in Figure 2.1.9 substitutes all occurrences of the word rs in a given string in $\{r, s\}^*$ with the symbol ★; if such a pattern does never occur, the output is undefined.

A couple of examples: the string $ssrrr$ is mapped to $\bot$, while the string $rrsrrrss$ is mapped to $r{\bigstar}rr{\bigstar}s$.

Using the epithet a-labelled for the arrows whose label is of the form $a/\dots$, the diagram above should be interpreted as follows:

- the set of states is $\{\heartsuit, \diamondsuit, \clubsuit, \spadesuit\}$;
- the input and the output alphabets are respectively $\{r, s\}$ and $\{r, s, \bigstar\}$;
- $\heartsuit$ is the initial state and ε is the initialization value;
- the partial termination function is undefined for $\heartsuit$ and $\diamondsuit$, while returns ε for $\clubsuit$ and r for $\spadesuit$;
- the transition function for r maps a state to the one its r-labelled outgoing arrow goes to, analogously for s;
- the production function for r maps a state to the word on the right part of the label of its r-labelled outgoing arrow, analogously for s.

2.2 Mathematical background for subsequential transducers

In this section, the notations and definitions useful to deal with minimal subsequential transducers are given.

Following Choffrut's philosophy in [8], a sort of extended monoid of words is defined, endowed with an action on itself.

Definition 2.2.1. A^* is a monoid with the operation of concatenation of words and with the empty word ε working as identity element.

It is actually the free monoid generated by A and may be referred to as the *monoid of words on* A.

Definition 2.2.2. $\overline{A^*}$, the extended A^*, is a monoid with the operation of concatenation of words, with the empty word ε working as identity element and with $\perp$ working as annihilating element:

$$v\perp := \perp =: \perp v \ \forall v \in \overline{A^*}.$$

It may be referred to as the *extended monoid of words on* A.

Now, the simple notions of length, prefix and suffix of a word should also be recalled, with the foresight of extending them to the new element $\perp$.

Definition 2.2.3. Let $w \in \overline{A^*}$.

Its *length* $|w| \in \mathbb{N} \cup \{\infty\}$ is defined as follows:

$$|w| := \begin{cases} \text{number of letters appearing in it} & \text{if } w \neq \perp; \\ \infty & \text{if } w = \perp. \end{cases}$$

Definition 2.2.4. An element $\widetilde{w} \in \overline{\Sigma^*}$ is said to be a *prefix* of $w \in \overline{A^*}$ if there exists $u \in \overline{A^*}$ such that $w = \widetilde{w}u$.

Definition 2.2.5. An element $\widetilde{w} \in \overline{\Sigma^*}$ is said to be a *suffix* of $w \in \overline{A^*}$ if there exists $u \in \overline{A^*}$ such that $w = u\widetilde{w}$.

For our scopes, only prefixes and their properties are addressed in the rest of the section.

Remark 2.2.6. If $x \in A^*$ and there exists a $w \in \overline{A^*}$ such that $y = xw$, such a w must be unique: if y is a word, it is because of how words are defined; if y is $\perp$, it is because w is forced to be $\perp$ too.

Definition 2.2.7. Let $w \in \overline{A^*}$; $\mathsf{Pr}(w)$ is the *set of prefixes of* w.

Remark 2.2.8. $\overline{A^*}$ with the relation $\sqsubseteq$ of being a prefix of, i.e.

$$v \sqsubseteq w \text{ if and only if } v \in \mathsf{Pr}(w)$$

with $v, w \in \overline{A^*}$, is a partially ordered set, whose minimum is ε and whose maximum is $\perp$.

In what follows, an important action is introduced.

Definition 2.2.9. The *minus action* is the function $\overline{A^*} \times \overline{A^*} \to \overline{A^*}$, $(x, y) \mapsto x^{-1}y$, defined as follows:

$$x^{-1}y := \begin{cases} w & \text{if } y = xw \text{ and } x \in A^*; \\ \perp & \text{otherwise.} \end{cases}$$

The minus action is well defined because of Remark 2.2.6. As a matter of notation, if $W \subseteq \overline{A^*} \ni x$, let $x^{-1}W$ denote the set $\{x^{-1}y \mid y \in W\}$.

Lemma 2.2.10. *The minus action introduced in Definition 2.2.9 is indeed a right monoid action.*

Proof. The two properties of identity and compatibility defining right monoid actions must be checked:

- $\varepsilon^{-1}z = z$ for all $z \in \overline{A^*}$;
- $y^{-1}x^{-1}z = (xy)^{-1}z$ for all $x, y, z \in \overline{A^*}$.

What could z be? If $z = \perp$, the action of the empty word on it returns $\perp$, otherwise the action of the empty word on z returns exactly z, so the first property holds.

Concerning compatibility, let's arbitrarily fix $x, y, z \in \overline{A^*}$ and let's consider two cases: the one in which $x, y \in A^*$ such that $xy \in \mathsf{Pr}(z)$ and the opposite one.

In the first case, $z = xyt$ with $t \in \overline{A^*}$:
$y^{-1}x^{-1}z = y^{-1}x^{-1}xyt = y^{-1}yt = t = (xy)^{-1}xyt = (xy)^{-1}z.$

In the opposite case, if either x or y is not a word, xy is not a word either and the equality holds as $\perp = \perp$; if they are both words, $y^{-1}x^{-1}z = \perp$, because even if x were a prefix of z, y surely would not be a prefix of $x^{-1}z$, as this would lead to the first case; in addition, $(xy)^{-1}z = \perp$ too, as the contrary would also lead to the first case.

This concludes the proof. □

Lemma 2.2.11. *Let W be a non-empty subset of $\overline{A^*}$. There exists a unique $w \in \overline{A^*}$ such that:*

$$w \in \cap_{x \in W} \mathsf{Pr}(x) \wedge \forall w' \in \overline{A^*} (w' \in \cap_{x \in W} \mathsf{Pr}(x) \Rightarrow |w'| \leq |w|). \tag{2.2.12}$$

Proof. First of all, notice that $\cap_{x \in W} \mathsf{Pr}(x)$ is not empty, as it contains ε.

If this intersection is a finite set, one can take a word whose length is maximal; if this intersection is not a finite set, the only possibility is that it is equal to $\mathsf{Pr}(\perp)$, and as $\perp$ belongs to it, one can take it; in both cases, the intersection contains no longer elements, so the condition (2.2.12) holds for such an element.

Now let's prove that it is unique, so suppose there exist w_1, w_2 satisfying (2.2.12).

Using the second conjunct of (2.2.12) firstly with $w = w_1, w' = w_2$ and secondly with $w = w_2, w' = w_1$, one easily gets that w_1 and w_2 have the same length.

If this length is ∞, they both are $\perp$.

On the contrary, w_1 and w_2 are words and are prefixes of all the elements in W, which is not empty; in addition, $W \neq \{\perp\}$, because otherwise $\perp \in \cap_{x \in W} \mathsf{Pr}(x)$ and $\infty = |\perp| \not\leq |w_1| < \infty$, so there exists at least one word $z \in A^*$ such that w_1 and w_2 are prefixes of z.

As w_1 and w_2 are prefixes of the same word and have the same length, they must coincide. □

Lemma 2.2.11 makes possible to state the following definition.

Definition 2.2.13. Let W be a subset of $\overline{A^*}$.

The *longest common prefix of* W, denoted by $\mathsf{lcp}(W)$, is defined as follows:

- if W is empty, $\mathsf{lcp}(W) := \bot$;
- if W is not empty, $\mathsf{lcp}(W) := w \in \overline{A^*}$ such that (2.2.12) holds.

Remark 2.2.14. Consider again $W \subseteq \overline{A^*}$.

$\mathsf{lcp}(W)$ is nothing but the longest element being a prefix of all the elements in W.

Coming back to Remark 2.2.8, the longest common prefix of W turns out to be the infimum of W in $\overline{A^*}$ with respect to the relation of being a prefix of.

In what follows, some easily provable properties.

Remark 2.2.15. If $X, Y \subseteq \overline{A^*}$ and $x, y, z \in \overline{A^*}$:

$$X \subseteq Y \Rightarrow \mathsf{lcp}(X) \sqsupseteq \mathsf{lcp}(Y); \tag{2.2.16}$$

$$\mathsf{lcp}(X) \sqsubseteq \mathsf{lcp}(Y) \Rightarrow \mathsf{lcp}(X \cup \{x\}) \sqsubseteq \mathsf{lcp}(Y \cup \{x\}); \tag{2.2.17}$$

$$x \sqsubseteq y \Rightarrow xx^{-1}y = y; \tag{2.2.18}$$

$$x \sqsubseteq y \Rightarrow x^{-1}(yz) = x^{-1}yz. \tag{2.2.19}$$

The following lemma correlates the longest common prefix and the minus action.

Lemma 2.2.20. *Let* $x \in \overline{A^*}$, $W \subseteq \overline{A^*}$, $x \sqsubseteq \mathsf{lcp}(W)$.

$$\mathsf{lcp}(x^{-1}W) = x^{-1}\mathsf{lcp}(W)$$

Proof. The thesis obviously holds if W is empty, so let's suppose $W \neq \emptyset$.

Concerning $x^{-1}\mathsf{lcp}(W)$ being the longest common prefix of $x^{-1}W$, it must be shown that condition (2.2.12) holds.

As $\mathsf{lcp}(W)$ is a prefix of all elements in W and $x \sqsubseteq \mathsf{lcp}(W)$, $x^{-1}\mathsf{lcp}(W)$ is a prefix of all elements in $x^{-1}W$ too.

If one takes another prefix of all the elements in $x^{-1}W$, let it be z, by definition xz is a prefix of all the elements in $xx^{-1}W$; nevertheless, $xx^{-1}W = W$ because $x \in \mathsf{Pr}(y)$ for all $y \in W$, so $|xz| \leq |\mathsf{lcp}(W)|$.

One can easily check that, having two elements v, w of the extended set of words such that $x \sqsubseteq v$ and $x \sqsubseteq w$, $|v| \leq |w|$ implies that $|x^{-1}v| \leq |x^{-1}w|$; in particular, $|x^{-1}xz| \leq |x^{-1}\mathsf{lcp}(W)|$; x may be a word or not, but in any case $|z| \leq |x^{-1}\mathsf{lcp}(W)|$.

This concludes the proof. □

What about considering the longest common prefix of a partial function into a set of words rather than the one of a subset of $\overline{A^*}$?

It suffices to take images into account.

Definition 2.2.21. Let $g\colon T \rightharpoonup B^*$ be a T-transduction.

The *longest common prefix of* g is defined to be the longest common prefix of the set whose elements are the images of g, in the sense of Definition 2.2.13:

$$\mathsf{lcp}(g) := \mathsf{lcp}(\cup_{t \in T} g(t)).$$

Lemma 2.2.20 and Definition 2.2.21 make possible to state the last two definitions of this section, whose idea is to decompose a T-transduction into a word, its longest common prefix, and an irreducible function.

Definition 2.2.22. A T-transduction $g\colon T \rightharpoonup B^*$ is said to be *irreducible* if $\mathsf{lcp}(g) = \varepsilon$.

Definition 2.2.23. Let $g\colon T \rightharpoonup B^*$ be a T-transduction.

The *reduction* of g is the T-transduction $\mathsf{red}(g)\colon T \rightharpoonup B^*$ such that for all $t \in T$:

$$\mathsf{red}(g)(t) := \mathsf{lcp}(g)^{-1} g(t).$$

Remark 2.2.24. The reduction of a T-transduction not nowhere defined is irreducible.

2.3 Minimal subsequential transducers

Definition 2.3.1. An SST accepting a subsequential transduction f is said to be *minimal* if there does not exist an SST accepting f with fewer states.

In the DFA case, a T-syntactic equivalence relation over $\mathcal{L}$ is introduced in order to describe minimal deterministic finite automata: something similar happens in the SST case, in which an analogous T-syntactic equivalence relation over a subsequential transduction must be introduced.

Definition 2.3.2. Let $f\colon A^* \rightharpoonup B^*$ be a transduction.

For all $u \in A^*$, a transduction $f(u-)$ can be defined as follows:

$$\begin{aligned} f(u-)\colon A^* &\rightharpoonup B^* \\ w &\mapsto f(uw). \end{aligned}$$

Moreover, for all $T \subseteq A^*$, a T-transduction can be defined as a restriction of such a transduction:

$$\begin{aligned} f(u-)|_T\colon T &\rightharpoonup B^* \\ w &\mapsto f(uw). \end{aligned}$$

Definition 2.3.3. Let $f\colon A^* \rightharpoonup B^*$ be a transduction, $T \subseteq A^*$.

The *T-syntactic equivalence relation over f* is defined as follows for all $x, y \in A^*$:

$$x \sim_T y \text{ if and only if } \mathsf{red}(f(x-)|_T) = \mathsf{red}(f(y-)|_T).$$

Notice that the dependence on T may not be pointed out if $T = A^*$.

As a matter of notation, let $Q/{\sim_T}$ denote the set Q quotiented by the T-syntactic equivalence relation over f, Q and T being two subsets of A^*:

$$Q/{\sim_T} = \{[u]_T \colon u \in Q\}.$$

If $Q = T = A^*$, the following notation is adopted for the syntactic equivalence relation over f:

$$A^*/\sim = \{[u] : u \in A^*\}.$$

Now, before introducing abstractly the minimal SST accepting a certain transduction, it may be remarked that, in general, a minimal SST is not defined up to renaming of states, as different SST accepting the same transduction may differ in how rapidly output symbols are computed, even if they have the same amount of states.

The following definition captures the idea of yielding successive output symbols as soon as possible.

Definition 2.3.4. An SST $(Q, A, B, q_0, t, u_0, (- \cdot a)_{a\in A}, (- * a)_{a\in A})$ is said to be *onward* if for all $q \in Q$:

$$\mathsf{lcp}(\cup_{a\in A}(q * a) \cup \{t(q)\}) = \varepsilon. \tag{2.3.5}$$

Onwardness guarantees the uniqueness up to renaming of states of the minimal SST, as shown by Oncina, García and Vidal in their joint work [17].

Theorem 2.3.6. *The minimal onward subsequential transducer accepting a subsequential transduction f is unique up to renaming of states.*

Example 2.3.7. The two SST in Figure 2.3.8 have the same amount of states and accept the same subsequential transduction; nevertheless, the one on the left is not onward, whereas the one on the right is.

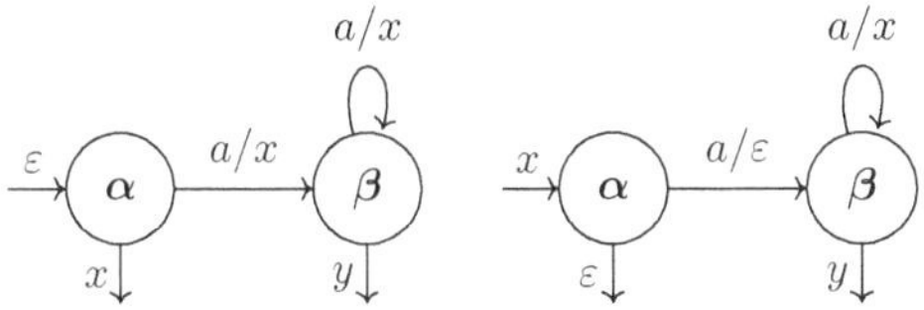

Figure 2.3.8. Not onward and onward subsequential transducers.

Example 2.3.9. It is easy to check that the subsequential transducer SSTex of Figure 2.1.9 is onward.

Before introducing the next proposition, a property linking undefined longest common prefixes to T-syntactic equivalence relations over f is needed.

Lemma 2.3.10. *For all $v, w \in A^*$:*

$$v \sim_T w \Rightarrow (\mathsf{lcp}(f(v-)|_T) = \bot \Leftrightarrow lcp(f(w-)|_T) = \bot). \tag{2.3.11}$$

Proof. As $v \sim_T w$, $\mathsf{lcp}(f(v-)|_T)^{-1}f(vt) = \mathsf{lcp}(f(w-)|_T)^{-1}f(wt)$ for all $t \in T$.

Let's suppose $\mathsf{lcp}(f(v-)|_T) = \bot$ and, by contradiction, $\mathsf{lcp}(f(w-)|_T) \neq \bot$: there exists $z \in T$ such that $f(wz) \neq \bot$, because of how $\mathsf{lcp}(f(w-)|_T)$ is defined.

In particular, $\bot = \mathsf{lcp}(f(v-)|_T)^{-1}f(vz) = \mathsf{lcp}(f(w-)|_T)^{-1}f(wz) \neq \bot$: a contradiction.

In conclusion, $\mathsf{lcp}(f(v-)|_T) = \bot \Leftrightarrow \mathsf{lcp}(f(w-)|_T) = \bot$, the converse obviously holding for symmetry. □

It is now possible to describe the minimal onward SST accepting a subsequential transduction f.

Proposition 2.3.12. *Up to renaming of states, the minimal onward subsequential transducer accepting f is the tuple*

$$(Q_{min}, A, B, q_0, t, u_0, (- \cdot a)_{a \in A}, (- * a)_{a \in A})$$

where:

- $Q_{min} = \{[u] \colon u \in A^* \wedge \mathsf{lcp}(f(u-)) \neq \bot\}$;
- *A and B are the initial and the final alphabets, according to f;*
- $q_0 = \begin{cases} [\varepsilon] & \text{if } \mathsf{lcp}(f(\varepsilon-)) = \mathsf{lcp}(f) \neq \bot, \\ \bot & \text{otherwise;} \end{cases}$
- $$\begin{aligned} t \colon Q_{min} &\rightharpoonup B^* \\ [u] &\mapsto \mathsf{red}(f(u-))(\varepsilon); \end{aligned}$$
- $u_0 = \mathsf{lcp}(f(\varepsilon-)) = \mathsf{lcp}(f)$;
- *for all $a \in A$*

$$\begin{aligned} - \cdot a \colon Q_{min} &\rightharpoonup Q_{min} \\ [u] &\mapsto \begin{cases} [ua] & \text{if } \mathsf{lcp}(f(ua-)) \neq \bot, \\ \bot & \text{otherwise;} \end{cases} \end{aligned}$$

- *for all $a \in A$*

$$\begin{aligned} - * a \colon Q_{min} &\rightharpoonup B^* \\ [u] &\mapsto \mathsf{lcp}(f(u-))^{-1}\mathsf{lcp}(f(ua-)). \end{aligned}$$

Remark 2.3.13. It is possible to verify that the described automaton satisfies Definition 2.1.5 and hence is a subsequential transducer, as long as its set of states is finite: let's check it.

- The defined set of states Q_{min} is supposed to be finite, by hypothesis; the independence from the choice of representatives is guaranteed by property (2.3.11), with $T = A^*$.
- A and B are the alphabets on which the sets of words of the subsequential transduction are defined.
- q_0 is either $\bot$ or belongs to Q_{min} independently from the choice of representatives, still as a result of property (2.3.11).
- $t \colon Q_{min} \rightharpoonup B^*$ is a trivially well defined partial function.
- $u_0 \neq \bot$ if and only if $\mathsf{lcp}(f) \neq \bot$ if and only if $q_0 \neq \bot$.

- The partial production function is well defined: if $u_1 \sim u_2$, $\mathsf{lcp}(f(u_1-))^{-1}f(u_1w) = \mathsf{lcp}(f(u_2-))^{-1}f(u_2w)$ for all $w \in A^*$; taking the longest common prefix of the union of the words starting with $a \in A$, one gets $\mathsf{lcp}(f(u_1-))^{-1}\mathsf{lcp}(f(u_1a-)) = \mathsf{lcp}(f(u_2-))^{-1}\mathsf{lcp}(f(u_2a-))$.
- The partial transition function is well defined: if $u_1 \sim u_2$, $\mathsf{lcp}(f(u_1-))^{-1}f(u_1w) = \mathsf{lcp}(f(u_2-))^{-1}f(u_2w)$ for all $w \in A^*$; taking only words starting with $a \in A$, $\mathsf{lcp}(f(u_1-))^{-1}f(u_1aw) = \mathsf{lcp}(f(u_2-))^{-1}$ $f(u_2aw)$ for all $w \in A^*$, true if and only if $\mathsf{lcp}(f(u_1-))^{-1}\mathsf{lcp}(f(u_1a-))$ $\mathsf{lcp}(f(u_1a-))^{-1}f(u_1aw) = \mathsf{lcp}(f(u_2-))^{-1}\mathsf{lcp}(f(u_2a-))\ \mathsf{lcp}(f(u_2a-))^{-1}$ $f(u_2aw)$ for all $w \in A^*$, see (2.2.18); because of the previous point, this means that $\mathsf{lcp}(f(u_1a-))^{-1}f(u_1aw) = \mathsf{lcp}(f(u_2a-))^{-1}f(u_2aw)$ for all $w \in A^*$, namely $u_1a \sim u_2a$; concerning the fact that $[u] * a$ should be defined if and only if $[u] \cdot a$ is, it is easy to check that $\mathsf{lcp}(f(u-))^{-1}$ $\mathsf{lcp}(f(ua-)) = \perp$ if and only if $\mathsf{lcp}(f(ua-)) = \perp$.

Thus, just one final preliminary result exactly about the finiteness of the set of states is needed before proving the proposition.

Lemma 2.3.14. *Let $f\colon A^* \rightharpoonup B^*$ be a transduction.*
f is subsequential if and only if the index of the syntactic equivalence relation over f is finite.

Proof. $\Leftarrow$) If the index of the syntactic equivalence relation over f is finite, the automaton described in Proposition 2.3.12, let it be S, is a subsequential transducer; in addition, it accepts f.

In fact, the following holds: $[S](a_1a_2\dots a_n) =$
$u_0(q_0 * a_1)(q_1 * a_2)\dots(q_{n-1} * a_n)t(q_n) = \mathsf{lcp}(f(\varepsilon-))\mathsf{lcp}(f(\varepsilon-))^{-1}\mathsf{lcp}(f(a_1-))\dots$
$\mathsf{lcp}(f(a_1\dots a_{n-1}-))^{-1}\mathsf{lcp}(f(a_1\dots a_n-))\mathsf{red}(f(a_1\dots a_n-))(\varepsilon) =$
$\mathsf{lcp}(f(\varepsilon-))\mathsf{lcp}(f(\varepsilon-))^{-1}\mathsf{lcp}(f(a_1-))\dots\mathsf{lcp}(f(a_1\dots a_{n-1}-))^{-1}\mathsf{lcp}(f(a_1\dots a_n-))$
$\mathsf{lcp}(f(a_1\dots a_n-))^{-1}f(a_1\dots a_n\varepsilon) = f(a_1\dots a_n)$.

$\Rightarrow$) Let's suppose that f is a subsequential transduction: as a consequence, there exists a subsequential transducer, let it be R, that accepts f.

Let Q_R denote the set of states of R, $|Q_R| < \infty$, and consider the partial function δ_R mapping words to the state reached through the transition function of R, that is:

$$\begin{aligned}\delta_R\colon A^* &\rightharpoonup Q_R\\ w = a_1\dots a_n &\mapsto (\dots((q_0 \cdot a_1)\cdot a_2)\dots)\cdot a_n.\end{aligned}$$

Clearly, δ_R returns $\perp$ if and only if any reached intermediate state is undefined.

Now consider two words $w_1 = a_1\dots a_n$ and $w_2 = a'_1\dots a'_m$ such that $\delta_R(w_1) = \delta_R(w_2)$: one gets that $w_1 \sim w_2$.

In fact, as a result of reaching the same state, the longest common prefixes of $f(w_1-)$ and $f(w_2-)$ share a common suffix, let it be k:
$\mathsf{lcp}(f(w_1-)) = u_0(q_0 * a_1)(q_1 * a_2)\dots(q_{n-1} * a_n)k$;
$\mathsf{lcp}(f(w_2-)) = u_0(q_0 * a'_1)(q'_1 * a'_2)\dots(q'_{m-1} * a'_m)k$.

Using the notation above, $q_i = q_{i-1} \cdot a_i$ and $q'_i = q'_{i-1} \cdot a'_i$, with $\delta_R(w_1) = q_n = q'_m = \delta_R(w_2)$ by hypothesis.

As a consequence, for all $w \in A^*$, $w = b_1\dots b_l$: $\mathsf{red}(f(w_1-))(w) =$
$\mathsf{lcp}(f(w_1-))^{-1}f(w_1w) = k^{-1}(q_n * b_1)(q_{n+1} * b_2)\dots(q_{n+l-1} * b_l)t(q_{n+l}) =$
$\mathsf{lcp}(f(w_2-))^{-1}f(w_2w) = \mathsf{red}(f(w_2-))(w)$, with $q_{n+i} = q_{n+i-1} \cdot b_i$.

As Q_R is a finite set and different equivalence classes are mapped to different elements of Q_R by δ_R, the index of the syntactic equivalence relation over f must be finite. □

Proof of Proposition 2.3.12. Remark 2.3.13 together with Lemma 2.3.14 guarantee that the presented automaton is a subsequential transducer accepting f: therefore, it remains to show that the presented SST is minimal and onward, the uniqueness up to renaming of states coming from Theorem 2.3.6.

Let's take another arbitrary SST, let it be P, accepting f and let's consider the map δ_P into its set of states, as defined in the previous lemma:

$$\delta_P \colon A^* \rightharpoonup Q_P$$
$$w = a_1 \dots a_n \mapsto (\dots((q_0 \cdot a_1) \cdot a_2) \dots) \cdot a_n.$$

Using the same reasoning as before, it is clear that $\delta_P(w_1) = \delta_P(w_2)$ implies that $w_1 \sim w_2$; in particular, $|Q_{min}| \leq |A^*/{\sim}| \leq |Q_P|$.

As the cardinality of the set of states of the presented SST is lower or equal than the one of the set of states of any other possible SST accepting the same transduction, minimality is guaranteed.

Concerning onwardness, let's consider an arbitrary $[u] \in Q_{min}$: $\mathsf{lcp}(\cup_{a\in A}([u]*a) \cup \{t([u])\}) = \mathsf{lcp}(\cup_{a\in A}(\mathsf{lcp}(f(u-))^{-1}\mathsf{lcp}(f(ua-))) \cup \{\mathsf{lcp}(f(u-))^{-1}f(u)\}) = \mathsf{lcp}(\mathsf{lcp}(f(u-))^{-1}(\cup_{a\in A}\mathsf{lcp}(f(ua-)) \cup f(u))) = \mathsf{lcp}(f(u-))^{-1}\mathsf{lcp}(f(u-)) = \varepsilon$, by means of Lemma 2.2.20.

This concludes the proof. □

2.4 Hypothesis subsequential transducers

Like in the L^*-algorithm, in the learning algorithm for SST the learner keeps in memory a couple (Q, T) of non-empty subsets of A^* such that Q is prefix-closed and T is suffix-closed; in particular, $\varepsilon \in Q \cap T$.

Using the translation queries and enlarging properly the two subsets, the learner may make the couple (Q, T) have the following three properties, whose definition makes use of the T-syntactic equivalence relation over f, f being the target transduction.

Definition 2.4.1. The couple (Q, T) is said to be *f-complete* if

$$\forall q \in Q \; \forall a \in A \; \exists \tilde{q} \in Q \colon \tilde{q} \sim_T qa.$$

Definition 2.4.2. The couple (Q, T) is said to be *f-correct* if

$$\forall q_1, q_2 \in Q \; \forall a \in A \; \forall t \in T \; (q_1 \sim_T q_2 \Rightarrow q_1 \sim_{T\cup\{at\}} q_2).$$

Definition 2.4.3. The couple (Q, T) is said to be *f-consistent* if

$$\forall q \in Q \; \forall a \in A \; \mathsf{lcp}(f(q-)|_T) \sqsubseteq \mathsf{lcp}(f(qa-)|_T).$$

In this way, the learner is able to produce an approximation of f, explicitly an hypothesis subsequential transducer associated to such a suitable couple.

Definition 2.4.4. Let (Q, T) be f-complete, f-correct and f-consistent.

The *hypothesis SST* associated to the couple (Q, T) is the automaton

$$(Q_{hyp}, A, B, q_0, t, u_0, (- \cdot a)_{a \in A}, (- * a)_{a \in A})$$

where:

- $Q_{hyp} = \{[u]_T \in Q/{\sim_T} \colon \mathsf{lcp}(f(u-)|_T) \neq \bot\}$;
- A and B are the initial and the final alphabets, according to f;
- $q_0 = \begin{cases} [\varepsilon]_T & \text{if } \mathsf{lcp}(f(\varepsilon-)|_T) \neq \bot, \\ \bot & \text{otherwise;} \end{cases}$
-
$$\begin{aligned} t \colon Q_{hyp} &\rightharpoonup B^* \\ [u]_T &\mapsto \mathsf{red}(f(u-)|_T)(\varepsilon); \end{aligned}$$
- $u_0 = \mathsf{lcp}(f(\varepsilon-)|_T)$;
- for all $a \in A$
$$\begin{aligned} - \cdot a \colon Q_{hyp} &\rightharpoonup Q_{hyp} \\ [u]_T &\mapsto \begin{cases} [ua]_T & \text{if } \mathsf{lcp}(f(ua-)|_T) \neq \bot, \\ \bot & \text{otherwise;} \end{cases} \end{aligned}$$
- for all $a \in A$
$$\begin{aligned} - * a \colon Q_{hyp} &\rightharpoonup B^* \\ [u]_T &\mapsto \mathsf{lcp}(f(u-)|_T)^{-1}\mathsf{lcp}(f(ua-)|_T). \end{aligned}$$

It is not trivial that the automaton in Definition 2.4.4 is a well defined subsequential transducer: the remaining part of this section is concerned with proving this fact.

The next lemma plays an essential role in proving that the cardinality of the set of states is finite.

Lemma 2.4.5. *Let T_1 and T_2 be two subsets of A^* such that $T_1 \subseteq T_2$.*

For all $v, w \in A^*$:

$$v \sim_{T_2} w \Rightarrow v \sim_{T_1} w. \tag{2.4.6}$$

Proof. Suppose $v \sim_{T_2} w$, that is, $\mathsf{lcp}(f(v-)|_{T_2})^{-1} f(vt) = \mathsf{lcp}(f(w-)|_{T_2})^{-1} f(wt)$ for all $t \in T_2$, the thesis being $v \sim_{T_1} w$.

If $\mathsf{lcp}(f(v-)|_{T_2}) = \bot$, one gets that $\mathsf{lcp}(f(v-)|_{T_1}) = \bot$ too because of (2.2.16), so the thesis clearly holds.

On the contrary, suppose $\mathsf{lcp}(f(v-)|_{T_2}) \neq \bot$ and hence $\mathsf{lcp}(f(w-)|_{T_2}) \neq \bot$, by property (2.3.11).

Let's take the longest common prefix of the two correlated sets, but just considering all t in $T_1 \subseteq T_2$:

$$\mathsf{lcp}\left(\bigcup_{t\in T_1} \mathsf{lcp}(f(v-)|_{T_2})^{-1} f(vt)\right) = \mathsf{lcp}\left(\bigcup_{t\in T_1} \mathsf{lcp}(f(w-)|_{T_2})^{-1} f(wt)\right). \quad (2.4.7)$$

Thanks to Lemma 2.2.20, (2.4.7) can be rewritten as follows:

$$\mathsf{lcp}(f(v-)|_{T_2})^{-1}\mathsf{lcp}(f(v-)|_{T_1}) = \mathsf{lcp}(f(w-)|_{T_2})^{-1}\mathsf{lcp}(f(w-)|_{T_1}). \quad (2.4.8)$$

Now, as $T_1 \subseteq T_2$, there exist $u_1, u_2 \in \overline{A^*}$ such that:

$$\mathsf{lcp}(f(v-)|_{T_1}) = \mathsf{lcp}(f(v-)|_{T_2})u_1 \wedge \mathsf{lcp}(f(w-)|_{T_1}) = \mathsf{lcp}(f(w-)|_{T_2})u_2.$$

Nevertheless, by virtue of (2.4.8):

$$u_1 = \mathsf{lcp}(f(v-)|_{T_2})^{-1}\mathsf{lcp}(f(v-)|_{T_1}) = \mathsf{lcp}(f(w-)|_{T_2})^{-1}\mathsf{lcp}(f(w-)|_{T_1}) = u_2.$$

Summing up, for all $t \in T_1$: $\mathsf{red}(f(v-)|_{T_1})(t) = \mathsf{lcp}(f(v-)|_{T_1})^{-1} f(vt) =$
$(\mathsf{lcp}(f(v-)|_{T_2})u_1)^{-1} f(vt) = u_1^{-1}\mathsf{lcp}(f(v-)|_{T_2})^{-1} f(vt) =$
$u_2^{-1}\mathsf{lcp}(f(v-)|_{T_2})^{-1} f(vt) = u_2^{-1}\mathsf{lcp}(f(w-)|_{T_2})^{-1} f(wt) =$
$(\mathsf{lcp}(f(w-)|_{T_2})u_2)^{-1} f(wt) = \mathsf{lcp}(f(w-)|_{T_1})^{-1} f(wt) =$
$\mathsf{red}(f(w-)|_{T_1})(t)$. □

Lemma 2.4.9. $|Q/{\sim_T}| \leq |A^*/{\sim}| < \infty$.

Proof. Lemma 2.3.14 states that $|A^*/{\sim}| < \infty$.

Now consider the function $\mu\colon A^*/{\sim} \to A^*/{\sim_T}$, $[v] \mapsto [v]_T$: it maps each equivalence class defined by the syntactic equivalence relation over f to the equivalence class of one of its representatives defined by the T-syntactic equivalence relation over f; μ is well defined because of Lemma 2.4.5, T_2 being A^* and T_1 being T.

As $Q \subseteq A^*$, it is true that $|Q/{\sim_T}| \leq |A^*/{\sim_T}|$; on the other hand, μ is clearly surjective, as a preimage of a certain element $[w]_T$ is simply $[w]$, hence $|Q/{\sim_T}| \leq |A^*/{\sim_T}| \leq |A^*/{\sim}| < \infty$. □

Corollary 2.4.10. *The set of states Q_{hyp} of the hypothesis SST is finite.*

Proof. Trivial. □

The next two lemmas are necessary to guarantee that the transition and the production functions are well defined.

Lemma 2.4.11. *Suppose that the couple (Q, T) is f-correct and f-consistent. For all $v, w \in Q$:*

$$v \sim_T w \Rightarrow$$
$$\mathsf{lcp}(f(v-)|_T)^{-1}\mathsf{lcp}(f(va-)|_T) = \mathsf{lcp}(f(w-)|_T)^{-1}\mathsf{lcp}(f(wa-)|_T)\ \forall a \in A. \quad (2.4.12)$$

Proof. Let's fix $a \in A$ arbitrarily.

As $v \sim_T w$, $v \sim_{T\cup\{at\}} w$ for all $t \in T$ thanks to f-correctness: using this fact together with f-consistency, one gets that $\mathsf{lcp}(f(v-)|_T)^{-1} f(vat) =$ $\mathsf{lcp}(f(w-)|_T)^{-1} f(wat)$ for all $t \in T$.

Finally, taking the longest common prefix of all these words, one gets that $\mathsf{lcp}(f(v-)|_T)^{-1}\mathsf{lcp}(f(va-)|_T) = \mathsf{lcp}(f(w-)|_T)^{-1}\mathsf{lcp}(f(wa-)|_T)$. □

Lemma 2.4.13. *Suppose that the couple (Q, T) is f-correct and f-consistent. For all $v, w \in Q$:*

$$v \sim_T w \Rightarrow va \sim_T wa \; \forall a \in A. \tag{2.4.14}$$

Proof. Let's fix $a \in A$ arbitrarily.

By hypothesis, $\mathsf{lcp}(f(v-)|_T)^{-1}f(vt) = \mathsf{lcp}(f(w-)|_T)^{-1}f(wt)$ for all $t \in T$ and hence $\mathsf{lcp}(f(v-)|_T)^{-1}f(vat) = \mathsf{lcp}(f(w-)|_T)^{-1}f(wat)$ for all $t \in T$ by f-correctness and f-consistency, the thesis being $\mathsf{lcp}(f(va-)|_T)^{-1}f(vat) = \mathsf{lcp}(f(wa-)|_T)^{-1}f(wat)$ for all $t \in T$.

By virtue of f-consistency and (2.2.18), notice that the equality $\mathsf{lcp}(f(v-)|_T)^{-1}f(vat) = \mathsf{lcp}(f(w-)|_T)^{-1}f(wat)$ for all $t \in T$ is true if and only if the equality $\mathsf{lcp}(f(v-)|_T)^{-1}\mathsf{lcp}(f(va-)|_T)\mathsf{lcp}(f(va-)|_T)^{-1}f(vat) = \mathsf{lcp}(f(w-)|_T)^{-1}\mathsf{lcp}(f(wa-)|_T)\mathsf{lcp}(f(wa-)|_T)^{-1}f(wat)$ for all $t \in T$ is: using Lemma 2.4.11, one may get the thesis. □

It is now possible to state the proposition for which this work has been done.

Proposition 2.4.15. *The hypothesis subsequential transducer associated to a couple (Q, T) being f-complete, f-correct and f-consistent is a well defined subsequential transducer.*

Proof. Let's check the properties a SST should have.

- The set of states is finite because of Corollary 2.4.10.
- A and B are the alphabets on which the sets of words of the subsequential transduction are defined.
- q_0 is either undefined or belongs to Q_{hyp}, as $\varepsilon \in Q$ and $[\varepsilon]_T \in Q_{hyp}$ if and only if $\mathsf{lcp}(f(\varepsilon-)|_T) \neq \perp$ if and only if $q_0 \neq \perp$ if and only if $q_0 = [\varepsilon]_T$.
- $t\colon Q_{hyp} \rightharpoonup B^*$ is a trivially well defined partial function.
- $u_0 \neq \perp$ if and only if $\mathsf{lcp}(f(\varepsilon-)|_T) \neq \perp$ if and only if $q_0 \neq \perp$.
- The partial production function is well defined, the independence from the choice of representatives coming from Lemma 2.4.11.
- The partial transition function is well defined, the image belonging to Q_{hyp} as a result of f-completeness and the independence from the choice of representatives being guaranteed by Lemma 2.4.13; concerning the fact that $[u]_T * a$ should be defined if and only if $[u]_T \cdot a$ is, it is easy to check that $\mathsf{lcp}(f(u-)|_T)^{-1}\mathsf{lcp}(f(ua-)|_T) = \perp$ if and only if $\mathsf{lcp}(f(ua-)|_T) = \perp$, by virtue of f-consistency.

□

2.5 The learning algorithm for SST

It is now possible to present the f^*-algorithm for learning subsequential transducers.

The algorithm takes as input a target subsequential transduction f and outputs the minimal SST accepting it.

First of all, the couple (Q, T) is initialized to $(\{\varepsilon\}, \{\varepsilon\})$; as long as this couple is not f-complete, f-correct and f-consistent, further words are added to the subsets Q and T to force these properties to arise, letting the reader build up an hypothesis SST.

If such an automaton still does not recognize the target transduction, then a provided counterexample and its prefixes are added to Q.

The algorithm works by performing these operations until the teacher agrees.

input : minimally adequate teacher of the subsequential target transduction f
output: minimal SST accepting f

$Q := T := \{\varepsilon\}$
repeat
    while *(Q, T) is not f-complete, f-correct and f-consistent* **do**
        if *(Q, T) is not f-complete* **then**
            add $qa \in QA$ s.t. $\nexists \tilde{q} \in Q \colon \tilde{q} \sim_T qa$ to Q
        end
        if *(Q, T) is not f-correct* **then**
            add $at \in AT$ s.t. $\exists q_1, q_2 \in Q \colon q_1 \sim_T q_2 \wedge q_1 \nsim_{T \cup \{at\}} q_2$ to T
        end
        if *(Q, T) is not f-consistent* **then**
            add $at \in AT$ s.t. $\exists q \in Q \colon \mathsf{lcp}(f(q-)|_T) \neq \mathsf{lcp}(f(q-)|_{T \cup \{at\}})$ to T
        end
    end
    ask an equivalence query for the hypothesis SST associated to the couple (Q, T)
    if *the answer is no* **then**
        add the provided counterexample and all its prefixes to Q
    end
until *the answer is yes*;
return *the hypothesis SST associated to the couple (Q, T)*

Algorithm 2.5.1. The *f^*-algorithm.*

Definition 2.5.2. A word w is said to be a *counterexample* for an hypothesis SST to accept a transduction f if the transduction accepted by the hypothesis DFA and the transduction f return different values for w.

Remark 2.5.3. Up to dissimilarities in presentation, the main difference between the presented algorithm and Vilar's may seem to lie in the properties the couple (Q, T) should have before exiting the while cycle and computing the associated hypothesis SST, as underlined in Figure 2.5.4.

f^*-algorithm	Vilar's algorithm
f-completeness	f-completeness
f-consistency	f-consistency
f-correctness	(2.4.12)
	(2.4.14)

Figure 2.5.4. Properties of (Q, T) in the f^*-algorithm and in Vilar's algorithm.

Nevertheless, it turns out that the conditions on the left are perfectly equivalent to the ones on the right; more precisely, the following result holds.

Proposition 2.5.5. *f-consistency $\wedge$ f-correctness $\Leftrightarrow$ f-consistency $\wedge$ (2.4.12) $\wedge$ (2.4.14).*

Proof. $\Rightarrow$) It follows from Lemmas 2.4.11 and 2.4.13.

$\Leftarrow$) Let's fix $q_1, q_2 \in Q$, $at \in AT$ arbitrarily and let's suppose that $q_1 \sim_T q_2$, the thesis being $\mathsf{lcp}(f(q_1-)|_T)^{-1} f(q_1\widetilde{t}) = \mathsf{lcp}(f(q_2-)|_T)^{-1} f(q_2\widetilde{t})$ for all $\widetilde{t} \in T \cup \{at\}$, by virtue of f-consistency.

The thesis clearly holds for $\widetilde{t} \in T$, so let's suppose $\widetilde{t} = at$.

By virtue of (2.4.14), it is true that $\mathsf{lcp}(f(q_1a-)|_T)^{-1} f(q_1at) = \mathsf{lcp}(f(q_2a-)|_T)^{-1} f(q_2at)$, and by virtue of (2.4.12), it is also true that $\mathsf{lcp}(f(q_1-)|_T)^{-1}\mathsf{lcp}(f(q_1a-)|_T)\mathsf{lcp}(f(q_1a-)|_T)^{-1} f(q_1at) = \mathsf{lcp}(f(q_2-)|_T)^{-1}\mathsf{lcp}(f(q_2a-)|_T)\mathsf{lcp}(f(q_2a-)|_T)^{-1} f(q_2at)$.

Using properties (2.2.18) and (2.2.19), one gets the thesis. □

2.6 Correctness and termination of the learning algorithm for SST

This section is devoted to prove the correctness and successful termination of the f^*-algorithm.

Let's first focus on the termination of the while cycle.

Proposition 2.6.1. *The while cycle terminates after a finite number of iterations.*

Proof. Let's define a counter associated to the couple (Q, T).

$$\mathbb{N}^3 \ni \left(|A^*/\sim| - |Q/\sim_T|, |Q/\sim_T| - |Q_{hyp}|, \sum_{\substack{q \in Q \text{ s.t.} \\ \mathsf{lcp}(f(q-)|_T) \neq \bot}} |\mathsf{lcp}(f(q-)|_T)| \right) \tag{2.6.2}$$

Lemma 2.4.9 guarantees that the first entry is a positive or zero number.

The goal is to show that the counter defined in (2.6.2) strictly decreases lexicographically after each execution of the while cycle.

- If line 5 or line 8 is executed, the first entry strictly decreases.

- If line 11 is executed, the first entry is fixed, whereas, letting q' be the element in Q witnessing the lack of f-consistency and at the word to add to T, either there exists $q \in Q$ such that $\bot = \mathsf{lcp}(f(q-)|_T) \neq \mathsf{lcp}(f(q-)|_{T\cup\{at\}})$ and the second entry strictly decreases, or the second entry is fixed and one has that $|\mathsf{lcp}(f(q-)|_{T\cup\{at\}})| \leq |\mathsf{lcp}(f(q-)|_T)|$ for all $q \in Q$ and $|\mathsf{lcp}(f(q'-)|_{T\cup\{at\}})| < |\mathsf{lcp}(f(q'-)|_T)| \neq \infty$; hence,

$$\sum_{\substack{q\in Q \ s.t. \\ \mathsf{lcp}(f(q-)|_{T\cup\{at\}})\neq\bot}} |\mathsf{lcp}(f(q-)|_{T\cup\{at\}})| < \sum_{\substack{q\in Q \ s.t. \\ \mathsf{lcp}(f(q-)|_T)\neq\bot}} |\mathsf{lcp}(f(q-)|_T)|$$

and the third entry strictly decreases.

As the canonical order on natural numbers is obviously terminating, the counter cannot decrease lexicographically forever: this means that the while cycle must terminate after a finite number of iterations. □

The number of equivalence queries that can be put in place is also limited.

Proposition 2.6.3. *Only a finite number of equivalence queries can be performed.*

Proof. Let's consider the couples (Q, T) and (Q', T'), the first one being the couple in memory immediately before operating an equivalence query and the second one being the couple in memory after operating the equivalence query unsuccessfully and making it f-complete, f-correct and f-consistent; notice that both of them are f-complete, f-correct and f-consistent couples.

The thesis is that $|Q/{\sim_T}| < |Q'/{\sim_{T'}}|$: that being the case, the number of performable equivalence queries must be finite, as the cardinality of these sets is bounded by the index of the syntactic equivalence relation over f (see Lemma 2.4.9).

By contradiction, suppose the thesis is false, that is, $|Q/{\sim_T}| = |Q'/{\sim_{T'}}|$, the inequality being excluded because of Lemma 2.4.5.

Because of the structure of the algorithm, this means that:

- $Q' = Q \cup \mathsf{Pr}(w)$, $w = w_1 \dots w_n$ being the given counterexample, as adding other words in Q would increase the cardinality;

- T' is the set T enriched only with words necessary to guarantee the f-consistency of the couple in memory, as adding other words in T would increase the cardinality.

Let H be the hypothesis SST associated to the couple (Q, T) and consider the value returned by the transduction accepted by H for the counterexample w: $[H](w) = [H](w_1 w_2 \dots w_n) = \mathsf{lcp}(f(\varepsilon-)|_T)\mathsf{lcp}(f(\varepsilon-)|_T)^{-1}\mathsf{lcp}(f(w_1-)|_T)$ $\mathsf{lcp}(f(q_1-)|_T)^{-1}\mathsf{lcp}(f(q_1 w_2-)|_T)\dots\mathsf{lcp}(f(q_{n-1}-)|_T)^{-1}\mathsf{lcp}(f(q_{n-1}w_n-)|_T)$ $\mathsf{lcp}(f(q_n-)|_T)^{-1}f(q_n) \neq f(w)$, with $q_{i-1}w_i \sim_T q_i$ for all $i \in \{1, \dots n\}$, $q_0 = \varepsilon$ and f being the target transduction.

The aim of the following part is to show that $[H](w)$ is indeed equal to $f(w)$, leading to a contradiction.

First of all, let's prove that the following hold:

$$q_{i-1}w_i \sim_{T'} q_i \ \forall i \in \{1, \dots n\}\,; \tag{2.6.4}$$

$$w_1 w_2 \dots w_i \sim_{T'} q_i \ \forall i \in \{1, \dots n\}\,; \tag{2.6.5}$$

$$w_1 w_2 \dots w_i w_{i+1} \sim_{T'} q_i w_{i+1};\ \forall i \in \{1, \dots n-1\}\,. \tag{2.6.6}$$

(2.6.4) easily follows from the supposed equality of cardinalities and the f-completeness of (Q', T').

(2.6.5) may be proven by induction: as $q_0 w_1 = w_1 \sim_T q_1$ is true, $w_1 \sim_{T'} q_1$ is true too, because of the supposed equality of cardinalities; if $w_1 w_2 \dots w_{i-1} \sim_{T'} q_{i-1}$, $w_1 w_2 \dots w_{i-1} w_i \sim_{T'} q_{i-1} w_i$ by means of (2.4.14), the property holding since (Q', T') is f-correct and f-consistent; but $q_{i-1} w_i \sim_{T'} q_i$, by means of (2.6.4).

(2.6.6) comes from (2.4.14) being applied to (2.6.5).

Now, (2.6.5) means that $\mathsf{lcp}(f(q_i-)|_{T'})^{-1} f(q_i t) = \mathsf{lcp}(f(w_1 \dots w_i-)|_{T'})^{-1} f(w_1 \dots w_i t)$ for all $t \in T'$; taking the longest common prefix of the two correlated sets, but just considering all t in $T \subseteq T'$, one gets that for all $i \in \{1, \dots, n\}$:

$$\mathsf{lcp}(f(q_i-)|_T) = \mathsf{lcp}(f(q_i-)|_{T'}) \mathsf{lcp}(f(w_1 \dots w_i-)|_{T'})^{-1} \mathsf{lcp}(f(w_1 \dots w_i-)|_T). \tag{2.6.7}$$

Analogously, but using (2.6.6), one gets that for all $i \in \{1, \dots, n-1\}$:

$$\mathsf{lcp}(f(q_i w_{i+1}-)|_T) = \\ \mathsf{lcp}(f(q_i w_{i+1}-)|_{T'}) \mathsf{lcp}(f(w_1 \dots w_i w_{i+1}-)|_{T'})^{-1} \mathsf{lcp}(f(w_1 \dots w_i w_{i+1}-)|_T). \tag{2.6.8}$$

Another important fact comes from (2.6.5) to which (2.4.12) is applied, the property holding as (Q', T') is f-correct and f-consistent, so for all $i \in \{1, \dots, n-1\}$:

$$\mathsf{lcp}(f(q_i-)|_{T'})^{-1} \mathsf{lcp}(f(q_i w_{i+1}-)|_{T'}) = \\ \mathsf{lcp}(f(w_1 \dots w_i-)|_{T'})^{-1} \mathsf{lcp}(f(w_1 \dots w_i w_{i+1}-)|_{T'}). \tag{2.6.9}$$

Putting (2.6.7), (2.6.8) and (2.6.9) all together and using the f-consistency of the two couples together with properties (2.2.18) and (2.2.19), one gets that $\mathsf{lcp}(f(q_i-)|_T)^{-1} \mathsf{lcp}(f(q_i w_{i+1}-)|_T) = \mathsf{lcp}(f(w_1 \dots w_i-)|_T)^{-1}$ $[\mathsf{lcp}(f(w_1 \dots w_i-)|_{T'}) \mathsf{lcp}(f(q_i-)|_{T'})^{-1} \mathsf{lcp}(f(q_i w_{i+1}-)|_{T'})$ $\mathsf{lcp}(f(w_1 \dots w_i w_{i+1}-)|_{T'})^{-1} \mathsf{lcp}(f(w_1 \dots w_i w_{i+1}-)|_T)] = \mathsf{lcp}(f(w_1 \dots w_i-)|_T)^{-1}$ $[\mathsf{lcp}(f(w_1 \dots w_i-)|_{T'}) \mathsf{lcp}(f(w_1 \dots w_i-)|_{T'})^{-1} \mathsf{lcp}(f(w_1 \dots w_i w_{i+1}-)|_{T'})$ $\mathsf{lcp}(f(w_1 \dots w_i w_{i+1}-)|_{T'})^{-1} \mathsf{lcp}(f(w_1 \dots w_i w_{i+1}-)|_T)] = \mathsf{lcp}(f(w_1 \dots w_i-)|_T)^{-1}$ $\mathsf{lcp}(f(w_1 \dots w_i w_{i+1}-)|_T)$ for all $i \in \{1, \dots, n-1\}$.

In particular, $\mathsf{lcp}(f(w_1 \dots w_i-)|_T) \sqsubseteq \mathsf{lcp}(f(w_1 \dots w_i w_{i+1}-)|_T)$, as a consequence of the equality above and the f-consistency of (Q, T).

Now, let's come back to the value returned by the transduction accepted by H for the counterexample w: $[H](w) = \mathsf{lcp}(f(\varepsilon-)|_T) \mathsf{lcp}(f(\varepsilon-)|_T)^{-1}$ $\mathsf{lcp}(f(w_1-)|_T) \mathsf{lcp}(f(q_1-)|_T)^{-1} \mathsf{lcp}(f(q_1 w_2-)|_T) \dots$ $\mathsf{lcp}(f(q_{n-1}-)|_T)^{-1} \mathsf{lcp}(f(q_{n-1} w_n-)|_T) \mathsf{lcp}(f(q_n-)|_T)^{-1} f(q_n) =$ $\mathsf{lcp}(f(\varepsilon-)|_T) \mathsf{lcp}(f(\varepsilon-)|_T)^{-1} \mathsf{lcp}(f(w_1-)|_T) \mathsf{lcp}(f(w_1-)|_T)^{-1} \mathsf{lcp}(f(w_1 w_2-)|_T) \dots$ $\mathsf{lcp}(f(w_1 \dots w_{n-1}-)|_T)^{-1} \mathsf{lcp}(f(w_1 \dots w_{n-1} w_n-)|_T) \mathsf{lcp}(f(q_n-)|_T)^{-1} f(q_n) =$ $\mathsf{lcp}(f(w_1 \dots w_{n-1} w_n-)|_T) \mathsf{lcp}(f(q_n-)|_T)^{-1} f(q_n)$; nevertheless, $q_n \sim_{T'} w_1 \dots w_n$ by virtue of (2.6.5) and hence $q_n \sim_T w_1 \dots w_n$ by virtue of Lemma 2.4.5, so $[H](w) = \mathsf{lcp}(f(w_1 \dots w_{n-1} w_n-)|_T) \mathsf{lcp}(f(w_1 \dots w_{n-1} w_n-)|_T)^{-1} f(w_1 \dots w_n) =$ $f(w_1 \dots w_n) = f(w)$, a contradiction as w is a counterexample for H to accept the target transduction f. □

Proposition 2.6.10. *The hypothesis SST associated to a couple (Q, T) being f-complete, f-correct and f-consistent is onward.*

Proof. Pick an arbitrary $[u] \in Q_{hyp}$: $\mathsf{lcp}(\cup_{a \in A}([u] * a) \cup \{t([u])\}) =$
$\mathsf{lcp}(\cup_{a \in A}(\mathsf{lcp}(f(u-)|_T)^{-1}\mathsf{lcp}(f(ua-)|_T)) \cup \{\mathsf{lcp}(f(u-)|_T)^{-1}f(u)\}) =$
$\mathsf{lcp}(\mathsf{lcp}(f(u-)|_T)^{-1}(\cup_{a \in A}\mathsf{lcp}(f(ua-)|_T) \cup f(u))) =$
$\mathsf{lcp}(f(u-)|_T)^{-1}\mathsf{lcp}(f(u-)|_{AT \cup \{\varepsilon\}})$ by means of Lemma 2.2.20, but as T is suffix-closed, $T \subseteq AT \cup \{\varepsilon\}$, so $\mathsf{lcp}(f(u-)|_T)^{-1}\mathsf{lcp}(f(u-)|_{AT \cup \{\varepsilon\}}) =$
$\mathsf{lcp}(f(u-)|_T)^{-1}\mathsf{lcp}(f(u-)|_T) = \varepsilon$. □

It is now possible to conclude with the most important result of this chapter.

Theorem 2.6.11. *The f^*-algorithm terminates and returns the minimal onward SST accepting the target transduction.*

Proof. Proposition 2.6.1 guarantees that each while loop the learner performs cannot go on forever and terminates after a finite number of iterations.

After exiting each while loop, the algorithm performs an equivalence query: if the answer is negative, a counterexample and its prefixes are added to Q, but this operation may happen just a finite number of times, by virtue of Proposition 2.6.3.

Therefore, the algorithm must terminate.

The only possible way the algorithm can terminate is by asking an equivalence query returning a positive answer: this means that the hypothesis SST associated to the latest couple accepts indeed the target transduction.

Moreover, the number of states of any possible hypothesis SST is lower or equal than the number of states of the minimal one accepting the target transduction.

Finally, the returned hypothesis subsequential transducer is onward, because any possible hypothesis SST is, by virtue of Proposition 2.6.10. □

2.7 Efficiency of the learning algorithm for SST

The efficiency of the extended algorithm in terms of time is analogous to the one of Angluin's.

Proposition 2.7.1. *The f^*-algorithm terminates in time polynomial in the size of the minimal SST accepting the target transduction f and the length of the longest counterexample returned by the teacher.*

As computational complexity is beyond the scope of this thesis, just an idea of the proof is given.

Proof (sketch). First of all, notice that the length of a word $f(w)$ is linear in the length of the word w: it is an easy consequence of the structure of subsequential transducers.

After adding a counterexample and its prefixes to Q, the index of $Q/\sim_T$ is increased at least by one: this means that the total number of equivalence queries is limited to the number of states of the SST accepting the target transduction, possibly increased by one (there may be just another element $[q] \in A^*/\sim$ not being a state, i.e. such that $\mathsf{lcp}(f(q-)) = \perp$).

Furthermore, an SST can be represented linearly in the number of states plus the number of arcs between states, times the maximum output word in an arc or a state; but the length of such a word is linear in the length of the maximum counterexample, so it is possible to ask an equivalence query in time polynomial in the size of the SST accepting the target transduction and the longest provided counterexample.

Let's now analyse the while cycle.

Concerning lines 5 and 8, each time a new value is added to Q or T the cardinality of $Q/\sim_T$ increases, so the total number of times these steps can be executed is bounded by the number of states of the SST accepting the target transduction, possibly increased by one.

Concerning line 11, the value of $|\mathsf{cp}(f(q-)|_T)$ decreases each time a new string is added to T and its length is a function being linear in the length of the words qt, hence the number of times this step can be executed is still polynomial in the length of the maximum counterexample returned and the size of the SST to learn.

As all the single steps individually considered just involve a number of operations being polynomial in the size of the SST to learn and the longest counterexample (see for instance the construction of the observation tables in the running example of Section 2.8), the proof is concluded. □

2.8 A running SST example

Let's illustrate the behaviour of the f^*-algorithm when it tries to learn the already met subsequential transduction $f\colon \{r, s\}^* \to \{r, s, \bigstar\}^*$, which replaces all occurrences of rs with $\bigstar$ and returns $\perp$ if such an occurrence does not appear; the input alphabet A is $\{r, s\}$, while the output alphabet B is $\{r, s, \bigstar\}$.

It is assumed that the length of the provided counterexamples is minimal.

For ease of calculation, it is useful to build up for each couple (Q, T) an observation table whose rows correspond to the elements in $Q \cup QA$ and whose columns correspond to the elements in T, such that the element in the position (m, n) is the image $f(\widetilde{q}t)$, with $\widetilde{q} \in Q \cup QA$ being the element corresponding to the mth row and $t \in T$ being the element corresponding to the nth column.

The couple with which the f^*-algorithm is initialized is the couple $(\{\varepsilon\}, \{\varepsilon\})$.

f	ε
ε	$\perp$
r	$\perp$
s	$\perp$

Figure 2.8.1. The observation table for the couple $(\{\varepsilon\}, \{\varepsilon\})$.

The observation table lets the learner easily compare either the reductions of the T-transductions associated to the elements in $Q \cup QA$ or the reductions of the $T \cup AT$-transductions associated to the elements in Q, in order to check f-completeness and f-correctness.

T	$\mathsf{red}(f(\varepsilon-)\vert_T)$	$\mathsf{red}(f(r-)\vert_T)$	$\mathsf{red}(f(s-)\vert_T)$
ε	$\bot$	$\bot$	$\bot$

Figure 2.8.2. The reductions of the T-transductions associated to $Q \cup QA$ for the couple $(\{\varepsilon\}, \{\varepsilon\})$.

The couple $(\{\varepsilon\}, \{\varepsilon\})$ is:

- f-complete, as r and s are T-equivalent to ε;
- f-correct, trivially, as Q consists only of ε;
- f-consistent, as $\bot = \mathsf{lcp}(f(\varepsilon-)|_T) \sqsubseteq \mathsf{lcp}(f(r-)|_T) = \mathsf{lcp}(f(s-)|_T) = \bot$.

Hence, the associated hypothesis SST is computed, but $\mathsf{lcp}(f(\varepsilon-)|_T) = \bot$, so it is the empty subsequential transducer and accepts the totally undefined transduction; this is not the target transduction, so a counterexample is given.

The given counterexample is rs, for which the target transduction returns $\bigstar$; the prefixes of rs are added to Q, so the new couple in memory is $(\{\varepsilon, r, rs\}, \{\varepsilon\})$.

f	ε
ε	$\bot$
r	$\bot$
rs	$\bigstar$
s	$\bot$
rr	$\bot$
rsr	$\bigstar r$
rss	$\bigstar s$

Figure 2.8.3. The observation table for the couple $(\{\varepsilon, r, rs\}, \{\varepsilon\})$.

T	$\mathsf{red}(f(\varepsilon-)\vert_T)$	$\mathsf{red}(f(r-)\vert_T)$	$\mathsf{red}(f(rs-)\vert_T)$
ε	$\bot$	$\bot$	ε

T	$\mathsf{red}(f(s-)\vert_T)$	$\mathsf{red}(f(rr-)\vert_T)$	$\mathsf{red}(f(rsr-)\vert_T)$	$\mathsf{red}(f(rss-)\vert_T)$
ε	$\bot$	$\bot$	ε	ε

Figure 2.8.4. The reductions of the T-transductions associated to $Q \cup QA$ for the couple $(\{\varepsilon, r, rs\}, \{\varepsilon\})$.

$T \cup \{s\}$	$\mathsf{red}(f(\varepsilon-)\|_{T\cup\{s\}})$	$\mathsf{red}(f(r-)\|_{T\cup\{s\}})$	$\mathsf{red}(f(rs-)\|_{T\cup\{s\}})$
ε	$\perp$	$\perp$	ε
s	$\perp$	ε	s

Figure 2.8.5. The reductions of the $T \cup \{s\}$-transductions associated to Q for the couple $(\{\varepsilon, r, rs\}, \{\varepsilon\})$.

The couple $(\{\varepsilon, r, rs\}, \{\varepsilon\})$ is f-complete: using Figure 2.8.4, it is easy to check that $\varepsilon \sim_T r \sim_T s \sim_T rr$ and $rs \sim_T rsr \sim_T rss$.

Nonetheless, the couple is not f-correct: $\varepsilon \sim_T r$, but $\varepsilon \not\sim_{T\cup\{s\}} r$, as one can see from Figure 2.8.5.

As a consequence, s must be added to T.

f	ε	s
ε	$\perp$	$\perp$
r	$\perp$	$\bigstar$
rs	$\bigstar$	$\bigstar s$
s	$\perp$	$\perp$
rr	$\perp$	$r\bigstar$
rsr	$\bigstar r$	$\bigstar\bigstar$
rss	$\bigstar s$	$\bigstar ss$

Figure 2.8.6. The observation table for the couple $(\{\varepsilon, r, rs\}, \{\varepsilon, s\})$.

T	$\mathsf{red}(f(\varepsilon-)\|_T)$	$\mathsf{red}(f(r-)\|_T)$	$\mathsf{red}(f(rs-)\|_T)$
ε	$\perp$	$\perp$	ε
s	$\perp$	ε	s

T	$\mathsf{red}(f(s-)\|_T)$	$\mathsf{red}(f(rr-)\|_T)$	$\mathsf{red}(f(rsr-)\|_T)$	$\mathsf{red}(f(rss-)\|_T)$
ε	$\perp$	$\perp$	r	ε
s	$\perp$	ε	$\bigstar$	s

Figure 2.8.7. The reductions of the T-transductions associated to $Q \cup QA$ for the couple $(\{\varepsilon, r, rs\}, \{\varepsilon, s\})$.

The updated couple $(\{\varepsilon, r, rs\}, \{\varepsilon, s\})$ is not f-complete: in fact, the word rsr is not T-equivalent to any of the elements in Q, so it must be added to the set (see Figure 2.8.7).

f	ε	s
ε	$\bot$	$\bot$
r	$\bot$	$\bigstar$
rs	$\bigstar$	$\bigstar s$
rsr	$\bigstar r$	$\bigstar\bigstar$
s	$\bot$	$\bot$
rr	$\bot$	$r\bigstar$
rss	$\bigstar s$	$\bigstar ss$
$rsrr$	$\bigstar rr$	$\bigstar r\bigstar$
$rsrs$	$\bigstar\bigstar$	$\bigstar\bigstar s$

Figure 2.8.8. The observation table for the couple $(\{\varepsilon, r, rs, rsr\}, \{\varepsilon, s\})$.

T	$\mathsf{red}(f(\varepsilon-)\|_T)$	$\mathsf{red}(f(r-)\|_T)$	$\mathsf{red}(f(rs-)\|_T)$	$\mathsf{red}(f(rsr-)\|_T)$
ε	$\bot$	$\bot$	ε	r
s	$\bot$	ε	s	$\bigstar$

T	$\mathsf{red}(f(s-)\|_T)$	$\mathsf{red}(f(rr-)\|_T)$	$\mathsf{red}(f(rss-)\|_T)$
ε	$\bot$	$\bot$	ε
s	$\bot$	ε	s

T	$\mathsf{red}(f(rsrr-)\|_T)$	$\mathsf{red}(f(rsrs-)\|_T)$
ε	r	ε
s	$\bigstar$	s

Figure 2.8.9. The reductions of the T-transductions associated to $Q \cup QA$ for the couple $(\{\varepsilon, r, rs, rsr\}, \{\varepsilon, s\})$.

As one can see from Figure 2.8.9, the new couple $(\{\varepsilon, r, rs, rsr\}, \{\varepsilon, s\})$ is f-complete; it is also f-correct, as there are no two different T-equivalent elements in Q.

Nevertheless, the couple is not f-consistent, as $\mathsf{lcp}(f(\varepsilon-)|_T) = \bot$ is not a prefix of $\mathsf{lcp}(f(r-)|_T) = \bigstar$: $rs \in AT$ is such that $\bot = \mathsf{lcp}(f(\varepsilon-)|_T) \neq \mathsf{lcp}(f(\varepsilon-)|_{T\cup\{rs\}}) = \bigstar$, so it is added to T.

The updated couple is hence $(\{\varepsilon, r, rs, rsr\}, \{\varepsilon, s, rs\})$.

f	ε	s	rs
ε	$\bot$	$\bot$	$\bigstar$
r	$\bot$	$\bigstar$	$r\bigstar$
rs	$\bigstar$	$\bigstar s$	$\bigstar\bigstar$
rsr	$\bigstar r$	$\bigstar\bigstar$	$\bigstar r\bigstar$
s	$\bot$	$\bot$	$s\bigstar$
rr	$\bot$	$r\bigstar$	$rr\bigstar$
rss	$\bigstar s$	$\bigstar ss$	$\bigstar s\bigstar$
$rsrr$	$\bigstar rr$	$\bigstar r\bigstar$	$\bigstar rr\bigstar$
$rsrs$	$\bigstar\bigstar$	$\bigstar\bigstar s$	$\bigstar\bigstar\bigstar$

Figure 2.8.10. The observation table for the couple $(\{\varepsilon, r, rs, rsr\}, \{\varepsilon, s, rs\})$.

T	$\mathsf{red}(f(\varepsilon-)\vert_T)$	$\mathsf{red}(f(r-)\vert_T)$	$\mathsf{red}(f(rs-)\vert_T)$	$\mathsf{red}(f(rsr-)\vert_T)$
ε	$\bot$	$\bot$	ε	r
s	$\bot$	$\bigstar$	s	$\bigstar$
rs	ε	$r\bigstar$	$\bigstar$	$r\bigstar$

T	$\mathsf{red}(f(s-)\vert_T)$	$\mathsf{red}(f(rr-)\vert_T)$	$\mathsf{red}(f(rss-)\vert_T)$
ε	$\bot$	$\bot$	ε
s	$\bot$	$\bigstar$	s
rs	ε	$r\bigstar$	$\bigstar$

T	$\mathsf{red}(f(rsrr-)\vert_T)$	$\mathsf{red}(f(rsrs-)\vert_T)$
ε	r	ε
s	$\bigstar$	s
rs	$r\bigstar$	$\bigstar$

Figure 2.8.11. The reductions of the T-transductions associated to $Q \cup QA$ for the couple $(\{\varepsilon, r, rs, rsr\}, \{\varepsilon, s, rs\})$.

It is easy to check from Figure 2.8.11 that the current couple is f-complete and f-correct, but still not f-consistent, as $\mathsf{lcp}(f(\varepsilon-)|_T) = \bigstar$ is not a prefix of $\mathsf{lcp}(f(r-)|_T) = \varepsilon$: $rrs \in AT$ is such that $\bigstar = \mathsf{lcp}(f(\varepsilon-)|_T) \neq \mathsf{lcp}(f(\varepsilon-)|_{T\cup\{rrs\}}) = \varepsilon$, so it is added to T.

The updated couple is hence $(\{\varepsilon, r, rs, rsr\}, \{\varepsilon, s, rs, rrs\})$.

f	ε	s	rs	rrs
ε	$\bot$	$\bot$	$\bigstar$	$r\bigstar$
r	$\bot$	$\bigstar$	$r\bigstar$	$rr\bigstar$
rs	$\bigstar$	$\bigstar s$	$\bigstar\bigstar$	$\bigstar r\bigstar$
rsr	$\bigstar r$	$\bigstar\bigstar$	$\bigstar r\bigstar$	$\bigstar rr\bigstar$
s	$\bot$	$\bot$	$s\bigstar$	$sr\bigstar$
rr	$\bot$	$r\bigstar$	$rr\bigstar$	$rrr\bigstar$
rss	$\bigstar s$	$\bigstar ss$	$\bigstar s\bigstar$	$\bigstar sr\bigstar$
$rsrr$	$\bigstar rr$	$\bigstar r\bigstar$	$\bigstar rr\bigstar$	$\bigstar rrr\bigstar$
$rsrs$	$\bigstar\bigstar$	$\bigstar\bigstar s$	$\bigstar\bigstar\bigstar$	$\bigstar\bigstar r\bigstar$

Figure 2.8.12. The observation table for the couple $(\{\varepsilon, r, rs, rsr\}, \{\varepsilon, s, rs, rrs\})$.

T	$\mathsf{red}(f(\varepsilon-)\vert_T)$	$\mathsf{red}(f(r-)\vert_T)$	$\mathsf{red}(f(rs-)\vert_T)$	$\mathsf{red}(f(rsr-)\vert_T)$
ε	$\bot$	$\bot$	ε	r
s	$\bot$	$\bigstar$	s	$\bigstar$
rs	$\bigstar$	$r\bigstar$	$\bigstar$	$r\bigstar$
rrs	$r\bigstar$	$rr\bigstar$	$r\bigstar$	$rr\bigstar$

T	$\mathsf{red}(f(s-)\vert_T)$	$\mathsf{red}(f(rr-)\vert_T)$	$\mathsf{red}(f(rss-)\vert_T)$
ε	$\bot$	$\bot$	ε
s	$\bot$	$\bigstar$	s
rs	$\bigstar$	$r\bigstar$	$\bigstar$
rrs	$r\bigstar$	$rr\bigstar$	$r\bigstar$

T	$\mathsf{red}(f(rsrr-)\vert_T)$	$\mathsf{red}(f(rsrs-)\vert_T)$
ε	r	ε
s	$\bigstar$	s
rs	$r\bigstar$	$\bigstar$
rrs	$rr\bigstar$	$r\bigstar$

Figure 2.8.13. The reductions of the T-transductions associated to $Q \cup QA$ for the couple $(\{\varepsilon, r, rs, rsr\}, \{\varepsilon, s, rs, rrs\})$.

The couple $(\{\varepsilon, r, rs, rsr\}, \{\varepsilon, s, rs, rrs\})$ is:

- f-complete, as

$$s \sim_T \varepsilon,$$

$$rr \sim_T r,$$

$$rss \sim_T rs,$$
$$rsrr \sim_T rsr,$$
$$rsrs \sim_T rs;$$

- f-correct, as there are no two different T-equivalent elements in Q;
- f-consistent, as

for ε
$$\varepsilon = \mathsf{lcp}(f(\varepsilon -)|_T) \sqsubseteq \mathsf{lcp}(f(r-)|_T) = \varepsilon,$$
$$\varepsilon = \mathsf{lcp}(f(\varepsilon -)|_T) \sqsubseteq \mathsf{lcp}(f(s-)|_T) = s,$$
for r
$$\varepsilon = \mathsf{lcp}(f(r-)|_T) \sqsubseteq \mathsf{lcp}(f(rr-)|_T) = r,$$
$$\varepsilon = \mathsf{lcp}(f(r-)|_T) \sqsubseteq \mathsf{lcp}(f(rs-)|_T) = \bigstar,$$
for rs
$$\bigstar = \mathsf{lcp}(f(rs-)|_T) \sqsubseteq \mathsf{lcp}(f(rsr-)|_T) = \bigstar,$$
$$\bigstar = \mathsf{lcp}(f(rs-)|_T) \sqsubseteq \mathsf{lcp}(f(rss-)|_T) = \bigstar s,$$
for rsr
$$\bigstar = \mathsf{lcp}(f(rsr-)|_T) \sqsubseteq \mathsf{lcp}(f(rsrr-)|_T) = \bigstar r,$$
$$\bigstar = \mathsf{lcp}(f(rsr-)|_T) \sqsubseteq \mathsf{lcp}(f(rsrs-)|_T) = \bigstar\bigstar.$$

Therefore, an hypothesis SST may be computed and an equivalence query may be performed.

The hypothesis SST associated to the couple $(\{\varepsilon, r, rs, rsr\}, \{\varepsilon, s, rs, rrs\})$ is the subsequential transducer

$$(Q_{hyp}, A, B, q_0, t, u_0, (- \cdot a)_{a \in A}, (- * a)_{a \in A})$$

where:

- $Q_{hyp} = \{[u]_T \in Q/{\sim_T} : \mathsf{lcp}(f(u-)|_T) \neq \bot\} = \{\varepsilon, r, rs, rsr\}$, denoting each state by the representative of the equivalence class it actually is in order to lighten the notation;
- A and B are the initial and the final alphabets;
- $q_0 = \varepsilon$;
- $$\begin{aligned} t\colon Q_{hyp} &\rightharpoonup B^* \\ \varepsilon &\mapsto \mathsf{red}(f(\varepsilon -)|_T)(\varepsilon) = \bot, \\ r &\mapsto \mathsf{red}(f(r-)|_T)(\varepsilon) = \bot, \\ rs &\mapsto \mathsf{red}(f(rs-)|_T)(\varepsilon) = \varepsilon, \\ rsr &\mapsto \mathsf{red}(f(rsr-)|_T)(\varepsilon) = r; \end{aligned}$$
- $u_0 = \mathsf{lcp}(f(\varepsilon -)|_T) = \varepsilon;$

•

$$-\cdot r\colon Q_{hyp} \rightharpoonup Q_{hyp}$$
$$\varepsilon \mapsto r,$$
$$r \mapsto r,$$
$$rs \mapsto rsr,$$
$$rsr \mapsto rsr,$$

$$-\cdot s\colon Q_{hyp} \rightharpoonup Q_{hyp}$$
$$\varepsilon \mapsto \varepsilon,$$
$$r \mapsto rs,$$
$$rs \mapsto rs,$$
$$rsr \mapsto rs;$$

•

$$-* r\colon Q_{hyp} \rightharpoonup B^*$$
$$\varepsilon \mapsto \mathsf{lcp}(f(\varepsilon-)|_T)^{-1}\mathsf{lcp}(f(r-)|_T) = \varepsilon,$$
$$r \mapsto \mathsf{lcp}(f(r-)|_T)^{-1}\mathsf{lcp}(f(rr-)|_T) = r,$$
$$rs \mapsto \mathsf{lcp}(f(rs-)|_T)^{-1}\mathsf{lcp}(f(rsr-)|_T) = \varepsilon,$$
$$rsr \mapsto \mathsf{lcp}(f(rsr-)|_T)^{-1}\mathsf{lcp}(f(rsrr-)|_T) = r,$$

$$-* s\colon Q_{hyp} \rightharpoonup B^*$$
$$\varepsilon \mapsto \mathsf{lcp}(f(\varepsilon-)|_T)^{-1}\mathsf{lcp}(f(s-)|_T) = s,$$
$$r \mapsto \mathsf{lcp}(f(r-)|_T)^{-1}\mathsf{lcp}(f(rs-)|_T) = \bigstar,$$
$$rs \mapsto \mathsf{lcp}(f(rs-)|_T)^{-1}\mathsf{lcp}(f(rss-)|_T) = s,$$
$$rsr \mapsto \mathsf{lcp}(f(rsr-)|_T)^{-1}\mathsf{lcp}(f(rsrs-)|_T) = \bigstar.$$

The described hypothesis subsequential transducer is depicted below.

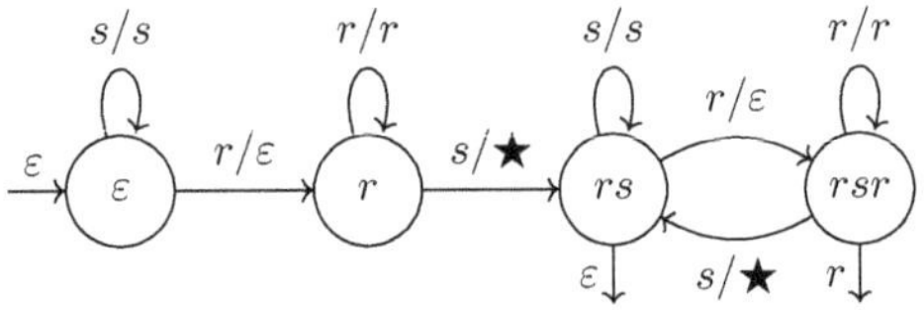

Figure 2.8.14. The hypothesis SST associated to the couple $(\{\varepsilon, r, rs, rsr\}, \{\varepsilon, s, rs, rrs\})$.

The hypothesis SST is exactly, up to renaming of states, the automaton SSTex of Figure 2.1.9 and accepts the target transduction: the equivalence query is answered positively and the algorithm terminates successfully.

Part II

Learning automata from a categorical perspective

Category theory takes a bird's eye view of mathematics.
From high in the sky, details become invisible,
but we can spot patterns that were impossible to detect
from ground level.

Tom Leinster,
Basic Category Theory,
2014

Chapter 3

A categorical approach for minimizing automata

Let's move a step forward the aim of this thesis: to present a unifying framework for learning a large class of automata, including deterministic finite automata and subsequential transducers, using the toolkit of category theory.

From this viewpoint, automata can be studied as functors from an input category to an output category.

First of all, some useful notions about factorization systems are recalled; secondly, automata as functors are formally presented; finally, the notion of minimal automaton, whose existence is guaranteed by some mild categorical properties, is captured categorically too.

To help the reader practice with the theory, some examples will be given, with particular reference to the well known deterministic finite automata; the more complex case of subsequential transducers, to which this thesis is dedicated, will be deeply taken into account in Chapter 5.

Except for the preliminary notions, which can be found e.g. in the related notes by Emily Riehl [19], this chapter is mainly based on the paper written by Professors Thomas Colcombet and Daniela Petrişan [10, 11], to which the reader should refer in order to have complete proofs.

3.1 Factorization systems

Definition 3.1.1. A *factorization system* in a category $\mathcal{C}$ is a pair $(\mathcal{E}, \mathcal{M})$ of distinguished class of morphisms such that:

- both $\mathcal{E}$ and $\mathcal{M}$ contain all isomorphisms and are closed under composition;
- every morphism f of the category $\mathcal{C}$ can be factored as $f = m \circ e$, with $e \in \mathcal{E}$ and $m \in \mathcal{M}$;
- the factorization above is functorial, that is, for all $e, e' \in \mathcal{E}$, $m, m' \in \mathcal{M}$ and u, v generic morphisms of $\mathcal{C}$ such that the diagram below commutes, there exists a unique arrow w such that both squares commute.

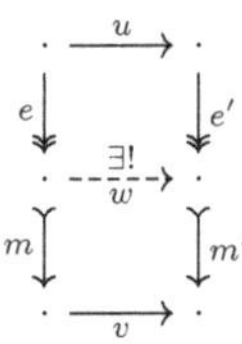

As a matter of notation, let $\longrightarrow\!\!\!\!\!\!\twoheadrightarrow$ denote the arrows belonging to $\mathcal{E}$, the *$\mathcal{E}$-quotients*, and let $\rightarrowtail$ denote the arrows belonging to $\mathcal{M}$, the *$\mathcal{M}$-subobjects*.

Example 3.1.2. A first, yet very meaningful example is the factorization system in Set $(\mathcal{E}, \mathcal{M})$ in which $\mathcal{E}$ is the class of surjective functions and $\mathcal{M}$ is the class of injective functions.

Remark 3.1.3. Two factorizations of the same morphism are isomorphic, that is, if $f = m \circ e = m' \circ e'$ with $m, m' \in \mathcal{M}$ and $e, e' \in \mathcal{E}$, then there exists a unique isomorphism n such that $m = m' \circ n$ and $e = n^{-1} \circ e'$.

In fact, using the functoriality of the factorization system, one gets the following commutative diagram, where $=\!=\!=$ denotes the identity morphism.

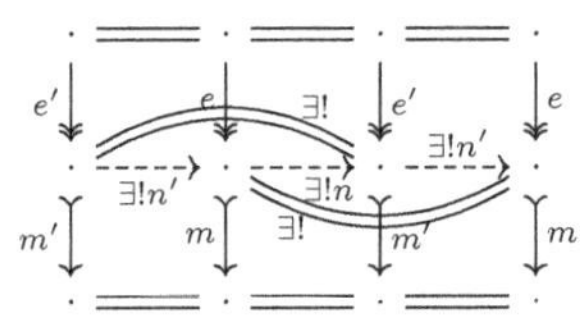

Using the uniqueness of the compositions, one gets that $n \circ n' = n' \circ n = id$, that is, n is an isomorphism and $n' = n^{-1}$; in particular, n is the unique isomorphism such that $m = m' \circ n$ and $e = n^{-1} \circ e'$.

Remark 3.1.4. The intersection of $\mathcal{E}$ and $\mathcal{M}$ is the class of isomorphisms of the category. Of course, all isomorphisms are included in such intersection by virtue of Definition 3.1.1; on the other hand, letting f belong to the intersection and using the functoriality of the factorization system, one gets that there exists a unique w such that $f \circ w = w \circ f = id$.

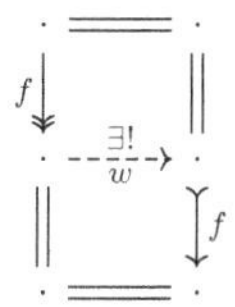

Clearly, f is an isomorphism and w is its inverse.

The following lemma turns out to be extremely helpful in the development of the discussion.

Lemma 3.1.5. *Let $(\mathcal{E}, \mathcal{M})$ be a factorization system of a category $\mathcal{C}$.*
$\mathcal{E}$ has the right cancellation property:

$$g \circ f \in \mathcal{E} \wedge f \in \mathcal{E} \Rightarrow g \in \mathcal{E}. \tag{3.1.6}$$

Dually, $\mathcal{M}$ has the left cancellation property:

$$g \circ f \in \mathcal{M} \wedge g \in \mathcal{M} \Rightarrow f \in \mathcal{M}. \tag{3.1.7}$$

Proof. Let's prove just the right cancellation property, the left one being dual.
Let $g \circ f \in \mathcal{E} \ni f$ and let's consider the factorization $g = m \circ e$: it suffices to check that m is an isomorphism to conclude.
Now one has two possible factorizations for the morphism $g \circ f$:

- $g \circ f = id \circ g \circ f$, with $id \in \mathcal{M}$ and $g \circ f \in \mathcal{E}$;
- $g \circ f = m \circ e \circ f$, with $m \in \mathcal{M}$ and $e \circ f \in \mathcal{E}$.

Because of Remark 3.1.3, the two factorizations are isomorphic, so there exists an isomorphism n such that $m = id \circ n = n$: in particular, m is an isomorphism. □

3.2 Languages and automata as functors

Let's consider an arbitrary small category $\mathcal{I}$, called the *input category*, and one of its full subcategories $\mathcal{O}$, denoting by i the inclusion functor: $\mathcal{O} \overset{i}{\hookrightarrow} \mathcal{I}$. Intuitively, $\mathcal{I}$ represents the inner computations performed by an automaton, and in particular its internal behaviour, while $\mathcal{O}$ represents the observable behaviour of the automaton and is used to define the language it accepts.
Another category to consider is the *output category* $\mathcal{C}$, which models the output computed by the automaton (e.g., a boolean value, probabilities, words over an alphabet).

Definition 3.2.1. A *$\mathcal{C}$-automaton* (or simply an automaton) $\mathcal{A}$ is a functor from $\mathcal{I}$ to $\mathcal{C}$. A *$\mathcal{C}$-language* (or simply a language) $\mathcal{L}$ is a functor from $\mathcal{O}$ to $\mathcal{C}$. A $\mathcal{C}$-automaton $\mathcal{A}$ *accepts* a $\mathcal{C}$-language $\mathcal{L}$ if $\mathcal{A} \circ i = \mathcal{L}$.
$\mathsf{Auto}(\mathcal{L})$ denotes the subcategory of the functor category $[\mathcal{I}, \mathcal{C}]$:

- whose objects are all $\mathcal{C}$-automata $\mathcal{A}$ accepting $\mathcal{L}$;
- whose arrows are *$\mathcal{C}$-automata morphisms*, meaning natural transformations $\alpha \colon \mathcal{A}_1 \Rightarrow \mathcal{A}_2$ such that $\alpha \circ id_i = id_{\mathcal{L}}$.

In this thesis, the input category $\mathcal{I}$ will be instantiated in two ways. The first one, $\mathcal{I}_{A^*}$, is used in [10, 11] to model different forms of *word automata*; in this section, it is described and used for modeling the running instantiation in the DFA case. Then, another input category will be considered, $\mathcal{I}_{Q,T}$, which will be used in the process of constructing a hypothesis automata.

Let's define now the input category $\mathcal{I}_{A^*}$, used for describing word automata. Here A is still a fixed finite alphabet and A^* is the set of words over it. The input category $\mathcal{I}_{A^*}$ is the category freely generated by the graph on the right, where a ranges over A. In other words, $\mathcal{I}_{A^*}$ is the three-object category with arrows spanned by $\triangleright$, $\triangleleft$ and a for all $a \in A$, so that the composition $\mathsf{st} \xrightarrow{w} \mathsf{st} \xrightarrow{w'} \mathsf{st}$ is given by the concatenation ww'. So, for example, the morphisms in $\mathcal{I}_{A^*}$ from in to st are of the form $\triangleright w$ with $w \in A^*$, while the morphisms on the object st are of the form w with $w \in A^*$.

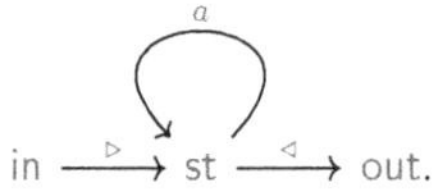

Let $\mathcal{O}_{A^*}$ denote the full subcategory of $\mathcal{I}_{A^*}$ on the objects in and out. Its morphisms are of the form $\mathsf{in} \xrightarrow{\triangleright w \triangleleft} \mathsf{out}$ for $w \in A^*$.

Hereafter, a language is meant to be a functor from $\mathcal{O}_{A^*}$ to $\mathcal{C}$ and an automaton is meant to be a functor from $\mathcal{I}_{A^*}$ to $\mathcal{C}$. If $\mathcal{L}(\mathsf{in}) = X$ and $\mathcal{L}(\mathsf{out}) = Y$, a language $\mathcal{L}$ will be referred to as a *$(\mathcal{C}, X, Y)$-language*; if $\mathcal{A}(\mathsf{in}) = X$ and $\mathcal{A}(\mathsf{out}) = Y$, an automaton $\mathcal{A}$ will be called a *$(\mathcal{C}, X, Y)$-automaton*. Two *running instantiations* of the output category $\mathcal{C}$ and of the objects X and Y will be provided: in this and in the next chapter, in order to model deterministic finite automata; in the last chapter, in order to model subsequential transducers.

Example 3.2.2. A deterministic finite automaton is a $(\mathsf{Set}, 1, 2)$-automaton. Indeed, a functor $\mathcal{A}\colon \mathcal{I}_{A^*} \to \mathsf{Set}$ with $\mathcal{A}(\mathsf{in}) = 1$ and $\mathcal{A}(\mathsf{out}) = 2$ can be seen as a DFA by interpreting

- $\mathcal{A}(\mathsf{st})$ as its set of states,
- $\mathcal{A}(\triangleright)\colon 1 \to \mathcal{A}(\mathsf{st})$ as choosing the initial state,
- $\mathcal{A}(a)\colon \mathcal{A}(\mathsf{st}) \to \mathcal{A}(\mathsf{st})$ as the transition map for the letter $a \in A$,
- $\mathcal{A}(\triangleleft)\colon \mathcal{A}(\mathsf{st}) \to 2$ as the characteristic map of the subset of accepting states.

Remark 3.2.3. A language in the sense of a subset of A^* can be identified in an obvious manner with a map from A^* to arrows of the form $1 \to 2$: this is the relation between a language in the categorical sense $\mathcal{L}\colon \mathcal{O}_{A^*} \to \mathsf{Set}$ and a language in the sense of a subset of words accepted by a deterministic finite automaton.

3.3 Minimization of automata

The aim of this section is to describe what it means to be minimal in a category, together with an abstract result of existence of such an object; then, sufficient material to cover the aforesaid two running instantiations is provided.

Definition 3.3.1. Consider two objects X, Y of a category $\mathcal{K}$. X $(\mathcal{E}, \mathcal{M})$*-divides* Y whenever X is an $\mathcal{E}$-quotient of an $\mathcal{M}$-subobject of Y, that is, there exists a span of the form:

$$X \twoheadleftarrow \cdot \rightarrowtail Y .$$

An object Z in $\mathcal{K}$ is $(\mathcal{E}, \mathcal{M})$*-minimal* if it $(\mathcal{E}, \mathcal{M})$-divides all the objects in $\mathcal{K}$.

As shown in the following lemma, having an initial and a final object turns out to be a sufficient condition for the minimal object to exist and be unique up to isomorphism.

Lemma 3.3.2. *Let $\mathcal{K}$ be a category endowed with an initial object I, a final object F and a factorization system $(\mathcal{E}, \mathcal{M})$. Let* Min *be the factorization of the unique arrow from I to F:*

$$I \twoheadrightarrow \mathsf{Min} \rightarrowtail F.$$

Then Min *is $(\mathcal{E}, \mathcal{M})$-minimal.*

Let's apply this lemma when $\mathcal{K}$ is instantiated with a category of automata $\mathsf{Auto}(\mathcal{L})$.

Corollary 3.3.3. *If the category $\mathsf{Auto}(\mathcal{L})$ has an initial automaton $\mathcal{A}_{init}(\mathcal{L})$, a final automaton $\mathcal{A}_{final}(\mathcal{L})$ and a factorization system, then the minimal automaton $\mathsf{Min}(\mathcal{L})$ for the language $\mathcal{L}$ is obtained via the following factorization:* $\mathcal{A}_{init}(\mathcal{L}) \twoheadrightarrow \mathsf{Min}(\mathcal{L}) \rightarrowtail \mathcal{A}_{final}(\mathcal{L})$.

Notice that this notion of minimization is parametric in the factorization system. A suitable factorization system on $\mathsf{Auto}(\mathcal{L})$ can be obtained from one on $\mathcal{C}$ as follows.

Lemma 3.3.4. *If a category $\mathcal{C}$ has a factorization system $(\mathcal{E}, \mathcal{M})$, then the category $\mathsf{Auto}(\mathcal{L})$ has a factorization system $(\mathcal{E}_{\mathsf{Auto}(\mathcal{L})}, \mathcal{M}_{\mathsf{Auto}(\mathcal{L})})$, where $\mathcal{E}_{\mathsf{Auto}(\mathcal{L})}$ consists of all natural transformations with components in $\mathcal{E}$ and $\mathcal{M}_{\mathsf{Auto}(\mathcal{L})}$ consists of all natural transformations with components in $\mathcal{M}$.*

The result of Corollary 3.3.3 can be specialized to the case of word automata $\mathcal{I}_{A^*} \to \mathcal{C}$. Due to the special shape of the category $\mathcal{I}_{A^*}$, the initial and the final automata may be computed, provided the output category satisfies some mild assumptions, recalled in Lemmas 3.3.5 and 3.3.7.

Lemma 3.3.5. *Fix a language $\mathcal{L}\colon \mathcal{O}_{A^*} \to \mathcal{C}$. If the category $\mathcal{C}$ has countable copowers of $\mathcal{L}(\mathsf{in})$, the initial automaton $\mathcal{A}_{init}(\mathcal{L})$ exists and is given by the following data:*

- $\mathcal{A}_{init}(\mathcal{L})(\mathsf{st}) = \coprod_{A^*} \mathcal{L}(\mathsf{in})$;
- $\mathcal{A}_{init}(\mathcal{L})(\triangleright)\colon \mathcal{L}(\mathsf{in}) \to \coprod_{A^*} \mathcal{L}(\mathsf{in})$ *is given by the coproduct injection corresponding to ε, for this reason this map will also be denoted by ε;*

- $\mathcal{A}_{init}(\mathcal{L})(a)\colon \coprod_{A^*} \mathcal{L}(\mathsf{in}) \to \coprod_{A^*} \mathcal{L}(\mathsf{in})$ *is given on the* w*-component* $\mathcal{L}(\mathsf{in})$ *by the coproduct injection corresponding to* wa*;*
- $\mathcal{A}_{init}(\mathcal{L})(\triangleleft)\colon \coprod_{A^*} \mathcal{L}(\mathsf{in}) \to \mathcal{L}(\mathsf{out})$ *is the coproduct of the morphisms* $\mathcal{L}(\triangleright w \triangleleft)\colon \mathcal{L}(\mathsf{in}) \to \mathcal{L}(\mathsf{out})$ *with* $w \in A^*$*, that is, it computes the value of the language on a given word, for this reason this map will also be denoted by* $\mathcal{L}?$.

Example 3.3.6. Since the category Set has all copowers, the initial automaton for a given language can be easily computed as an instance of the above lemma.

$$1 \xrightarrow{\ \varepsilon\ } A^* \xrightarrow{\ \mathcal{L}?\ } 2 \qquad (\text{loop on } A^*:\ w \mapsto wa)$$

Given a language $\mathcal{L}\colon \mathcal{O}_{A^*} \to \mathsf{Set}$, the initial deterministic automaton accepting $\mathcal{L}$ is described above in the diagram. Its state space is the set of all words, with ε being the initial one. A word is accepted if and only if it belongs to the language.

Lemma 3.3.7. *Fix a language* $\mathcal{L}\colon \mathcal{O}_{A^*} \to \mathcal{C}$*. If the category* $\mathcal{C}$ *has countable powers of* $\mathcal{L}(\mathsf{out})$*, the final automaton* $\mathcal{A}_{final}(\mathcal{L})$ *exists and is given by the following data:*

- $\mathcal{A}_{final}(\mathcal{L})(\mathsf{st}) = \prod_{A^*} \mathcal{L}(\mathsf{out})$*;*
- $\mathcal{A}_{final}(\mathcal{L})(\triangleright)\colon \mathcal{L}(\mathsf{in}) \to \prod_{A^*} \mathcal{L}(\mathsf{out})$ *is the product of the morphisms* $\mathcal{L}(\triangleright w \triangleleft)\colon \mathcal{L}(\mathsf{in}) \to \mathcal{L}(\mathsf{out})$ *with* $w \in A^*$*, for this reason this map will also be denoted by* $\mathcal{L}$*;*
- $\mathcal{A}_{final}(\mathcal{L})(a)\colon \prod_{A^*} \mathcal{L}(\mathsf{out}) \to \prod_{A^*} \mathcal{L}(\mathsf{out})$ *is the product over* $w \in A^*$ *of the* aw*-projections* $\prod_{A^*} \mathcal{L}(\mathsf{out}) \to \mathcal{L}(\mathsf{out})$*;*
- $\mathcal{A}_{final}(\mathcal{L})(\triangleleft)\colon \prod_{A^*} \mathcal{L}(\mathsf{out}) \to \mathcal{L}(\mathsf{out})$ *is given by the* ε*-projection, for this reason this map will also be denoted by* $\varepsilon?$.

Example 3.3.8. Since the category Set has all powers, the final automaton for a given language can be computed using the lemma above.

$$1 \xrightarrow{\ \mathcal{L}\ } 2^{A^*} \xrightarrow{\ K \mapsto K(\varepsilon)\ } 2 \qquad (\text{loop on } 2^{A^*}:\ K \mapsto a^{-1}K)$$

Given a language $\mathcal{L}\colon \mathcal{O}_{A^*} \to \mathsf{Set}$, the final deterministic automaton accepting $\mathcal{L}$ is described above. Its state space is the set of all languages over the alphabet A. The initial state is the language $\mathcal{L}$ itself. A language is an accepting state if and only if it contains ε. Given a language K, while reading letter a, the automaton goes to the residual language $a^{-1}K = \{u \in K \mid au \in K\}$.

Combining Corollary 3.3.3 with the three lemmas above, one has the following.

Theorem 3.3.9. *Let $\mathcal{C}$ be a category with a factorization system $(\mathcal{E}, \mathcal{M})$ and let $\mathcal{L}\colon \mathcal{O}_{A^*} \to \mathcal{C}$ be a language. Suppose $\mathcal{C}$ has all countable copowers of $\mathcal{L}(\mathsf{in})$ and all countable powers of $\mathcal{L}(\mathsf{out})$. The minimal $\mathcal{C}$-automaton $\mathsf{Min}(\mathcal{L})$ accepting $\mathcal{L}$ is obtained via the factorization in the commuting diagram to the right.*

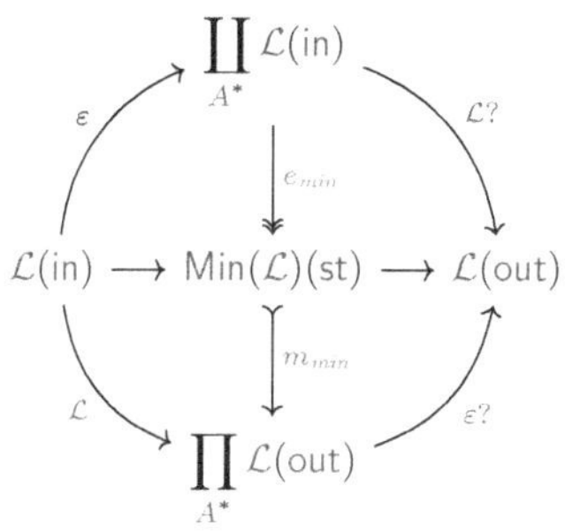

Example 3.3.10. Let's see how Theorem 3.3.9 instantiates in the case of deterministic finite automata for a given language $\mathcal{L}\colon \mathcal{O}_{A^*} \to \mathsf{Set}$.

Recall that such a functor may be interpreted as a language $\mathcal{L}$ in the sense of a subset of A^* (see Remark 3.2.3).

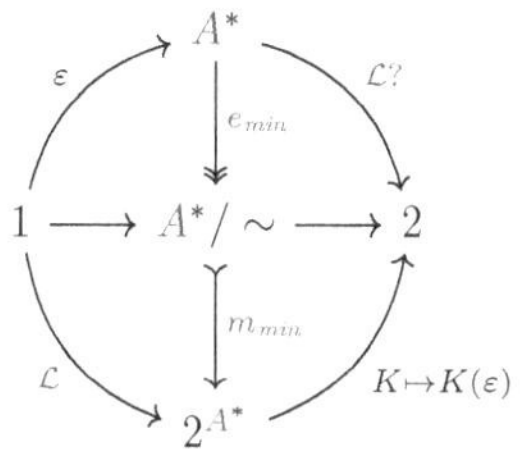

The only arrow from A^* to 2^{A^*} making the diagram commute maps an element $w \in A^*$ to the residual language $w^{-1}\mathcal{L} = \{v \in A^* \mid wv \in \mathcal{L}\}$; the factorization of such a map:

- first maps an element $w \in A^*$ to its equivalence class according to the syntactic equivalence relation over $\mathcal{L}$ defined in Section 1.2;
- secondly maps an equivalence class $[w]$ to the residual language $w^{-1}\mathcal{L}$.

The minimal deterministic finite automaton accepting $\mathcal{L}$ is depicted below in detail.

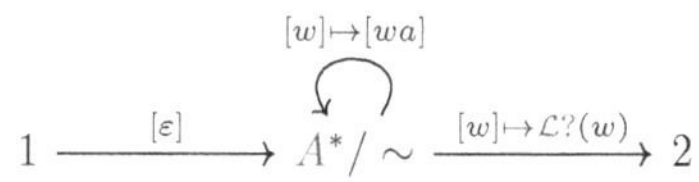

As one can see, the automaton turns out to be the minimal DFA described in Proposition 1.2.4, as long as the language to learn is regular, that is, the index of the syntactic equivalence relation over $\mathcal{L}$, corresponding to the cardinality of the set of states, is finite.

Chapter 4

A categorical approach for learning automata

In this chapter, the generic FunL*-algorithm for learning word automata, originally presented in the research article written by the author and the supervisors [9], is finally provided.

Just as in Angluin's algorithm, there are a teacher and a learner. Throughout this section, the alphabet A, the output category $\mathcal{C}$ and its factorization system $(\mathcal{E}, \mathcal{M})$ are fixed and known to both teacher and learner. The teacher knows a language $\mathcal{L}\colon \mathcal{O}_{A^*} \to \mathcal{C}$, hereafter called the *target language*. The learner wants to find this language, the output of the algorithm being the minimal automaton $\mathsf{Min}(\mathcal{L})$ accepting $\mathcal{L}$. The learner can ask the two following kinds of queries, which can be thought as high-level generalizations of Angluin's original ones in the special case of deterministic automata (see [1]).

- *Evaluation queries*: given a certain word w, what is $\mathcal{L}(\triangleright w \triangleleft)$?
- *Equivalence queries*: does a certain automaton accept the target language? If it does not, what is a counterexample for it not doing that?

In order to formulate the generic algorithm, the notions of table and hypothesis automaton from Angluin's original algorithm must be generalized. This is done in Section 4.1. The generic algorithm is provided together with its correctness and termination in Section 4.2. An optimized version of the learning algorithm is finally provided in Section 4.3.

4.1 Hypothesis automata

Just as in Angluin's L^*-algorithm, the learner keeps in memory a pair (Q, T) of subsets of A^* such that Q is prefix-closed, i.e. it contains the prefixes of all its elements, while T is suffix-closed, the same for the suffixes; in particular, $\varepsilon \in Q \cap T$. Using the evaluation queries, the learner produces an approximation of $\mathsf{Min}(\mathcal{L})$, explicitly a hypothesis automaton, to be introduced in Definition 4.1.8.

It turns out that the category $\mathsf{Auto}(\mathcal{L})$ does not suffice to capture the whole learning process. At a given stage of the algorithm, the learner has access, via evaluation queries, only to a part of $\mathcal{L}$: specifically, he knows the values of $\mathcal{L}(\triangleright qt\triangleleft)$ and $\mathcal{L}(\triangleright qat\triangleleft)$, where $q \in Q$, $t \in T$ and $a \in A$. This leads to consider a restriction of the language $\mathcal{L}$ to a subcategory of $\mathcal{O}_{A^*}$ whose arrows are of the form $\triangleright qt\triangleleft$ or $\triangleright qat\triangleleft$ as above.

To produce a hypothesis automaton consistent with this partial view of $\mathcal{L}$, the input category should be adapted too. A first attempt would be to discard some of the arrows of $\mathcal{I}_{A^*}$ from in to st, respectively from st to out. Explicitly, it would be likable to keep only the arrows of the form $\triangleright q\colon \mathsf{in} \to \mathsf{st}$ for the state words $q \in Q$ and, respectively, $t\triangleleft\colon \mathsf{st} \to \mathsf{out}$ for the test words $t \in T$. However, this is not feasible: the transition maps $a\colon \mathsf{st} \to \mathsf{st}$ would also be needed and via composition, for example, all arrows $\triangleright w\colon \mathsf{in} \to \mathsf{st}$ would be generated. The solution is to dissociate the state object st in $\mathcal{I}_{A^*}$ and consider a four-state input category.

Definition 4.1.1. The input category $\mathcal{I}_{Q,T}$ is the free category generated by the graph

$$\mathsf{in} \xrightarrow{\triangleright q} \mathsf{st}_1 \underset{\varepsilon}{\overset{a}{\rightrightarrows}} \mathsf{st}_2 \xrightarrow{t\triangleleft} \mathsf{out}$$

for all $q \in Q$, $a \in A$, $t \in T$ and with ε a fixed symbol (informally representing the empty word) such that the following *coherence diagrams* commute for all $a \in A$, for all $q \in Q$ such that $qa \in Q$, and for all $t \in T$ such that $at \in T$:

$$\begin{array}{ccccc} & & \mathsf{st}_1 & & \\ & \nearrow^{\triangleright q} & & \searrow^{a} & \\ \mathsf{in} & & & & \mathsf{st}_2; \\ & \searrow_{\triangleright qa} & & \nearrow_{\varepsilon} & \\ & & \mathsf{st}_1 & & \end{array} \qquad \begin{array}{ccccc} & & \mathsf{st}_2 & & \\ & \nearrow^{a} & & \searrow^{t\triangleleft} & \\ \mathsf{st}_1 & & & & \mathsf{out}. \\ & \searrow_{\varepsilon} & & \nearrow_{at\triangleleft} & \\ & & \mathsf{st}_2 & & \end{array}$$

Furthermore, let $\mathcal{O}_{Q,T}$ denote the full subcategory of $\mathcal{I}_{Q,T}$ on the objects in and out.

The two coherence diagrams in the definition of $\mathcal{I}_{Q,T}$, as well as the prefix-closure of Q and the suffix-closure of T, ensure that there is a functor

$$i^*\colon \mathcal{I}_{Q,T} \to \mathcal{I}_{A^*}$$

which merges st_1 and st_2 sending both of them to st, maps $\varepsilon\colon \mathsf{st}_1 \to \mathsf{st}_2$ to the identity on st and maps all the other morphisms of $\mathcal{I}_{Q,T}$ to the homonymous ones in $\mathcal{I}_{A^*}$.

As a matter of notation, given a coproduct $\coprod_{i\in I} X_i$ and arrows $f_i\colon X_i \to Y$, let $\coprod_{i\in I} f_i$ denote the mediating arrow $\coprod_{i\in I} X_i \to Y$ obtained from the universal property and let $\prod_{i\in I} g_i\colon X \to \prod_{i\in I} Y_i$ be defined dually for a family of morphisms $g_i\colon X \to Y_i$.

Lemma 4.1.2. *The functor* $i^*: \mathcal{I}_{Q,T} \to \mathcal{I}_{A^*}$ *is well defined and, furthermore,* $\mathcal{O}_{Q,T}$ *is a subcategory of* $\mathcal{O}_{A^*}$. *That is, the following diagram commutes:*

$$\begin{array}{ccc} \mathcal{O}_{Q,T} & \hookrightarrow & \mathcal{O}_{A^*} \\ \downarrow & & \downarrow \\ \mathcal{I}_{Q,T} & \xrightarrow{i^*} & \mathcal{I}_{A^*}. \end{array}$$

Proof. Let's just show that $\mathcal{O}_{Q,T}$ is a subcategory of $\mathcal{O}_{A^*}$: the fact that i^* is well defined is proved analogously. To this end, let's check that, for every word w resulting from the sequential concatenation of words in Q, A and T, there is only an arrow $\triangleright w \triangleleft$ in $\mathcal{O}_{Q,T}$. The coherence diagrams in the definition of the category $\mathcal{I}_{Q,T}$ are needed, see Definition 4.1.1.

Suppose there are two ways of getting w as above, qat and $q'a't'$: let's check that $\triangleright qat \triangleleft = \triangleright q'a't' \triangleleft$.

Assume $q = q_1 \dots q_n$, $q' = q'_1 \dots q'_{n'}$, $t = t_1 \dots t_m$, $t' = t'_1 \dots t'_{m'}$, where $q_i, q'_i, t_i, t'_i \in A$ are letters.

Without loss of generality, suppose that q is a prefix of q'; by induction, one gets that $(\triangleright q_1 \dots q_n)a(t_1 \dots t_m \triangleleft) = (\triangleright q_1 \dots q_n a)\varepsilon(t_1 \dots t_m \triangleleft) =$
$(\triangleright q_1 \dots q_n a)t_1(t_2 \dots t_m \triangleleft) = (\triangleright q_1 \dots q_n a t_1)\varepsilon(t_2 \dots t_m \triangleleft) = \dots =$
$(\triangleright q'_1 \dots q'_{n'})a'(t'_1 \dots t'_{m'} \triangleleft)$, as desired.

Notice that prefix-closure of Q and suffix-closure of T have been essential in order to properly use the coherence diagrams. □

The partial knowledge of the language $\mathcal{L}$ the learner has access to at this given stage of the algorithm is captured by the restriction $\mathcal{L}_{Q,T}$ of $\mathcal{L}$ to $\mathcal{O}_{Q,T}$:

$$\mathcal{L}_{Q,T}: \mathcal{O}_{Q,T} \hookrightarrow \mathcal{O}_{A^*} \xrightarrow{\mathcal{L}} \mathcal{C}.$$

Hence, to a pair (Q,T) can be associated the category $\mathsf{Auto}(\mathcal{L}_{Q,T})$, obtained by instantiating in Definition 3.2.1 the input category $\mathcal{I}$ with $\mathcal{I}_{Q,T}$ and its observable behaviour subcategory with $\mathcal{O}_{Q,T} \hookrightarrow \mathcal{I}_{Q,T}$.

Definition 4.1.3. A functor $\mathcal{B}$ in $\mathsf{Auto}(\mathcal{L}_{Q,T})$ is said to be a *(Q,T)-biautomaton* or a *$\mathcal{C}_{Q,T}$-biautomaton*, if the dependence on $\mathcal{C}$ has to be underlined. $\mathcal{B}$ is said to be *consistent* with the $\mathcal{C}$-language $\mathcal{L}$.

In the L^*-algorithm, the learner constructs a table associated to each pair of subsets (Q,T). This is done essentially by computing the quotient of the state words in Q by an approximation $\sim_T$ of the Myhill-Nerode equivalence for a language $\mathcal{L}$ given by: $w \sim_T v$ if and only if for all $t \in T$ one has $wt \in \mathcal{L} \Leftrightarrow vt \in \mathcal{L}$.

This leads to consider as a generalization of the notion of *table* the *minimal biautomaton* $\mathsf{Min}(\mathcal{L}_{Q,T})$ in the category $\mathsf{Auto}(\mathcal{L}_{Q,T})$. In order to compute it, Corollary 3.3.3 may be used. To this end, first the initial and the final objects of $\mathsf{Auto}(\mathcal{L}_{Q,T})$ are exhibited explicitly, assuming that the output category $\mathcal{C}$ has got certain products and coproducts.

The following notation will be used: given two subsets R and S of A^*, let RS denote the set $\{xy \mid x \in R, y \in S\}$.

Lemma 4.1.4. *Assume* $\mathcal{C}$ *has all countable copowers of* $\mathcal{L}(\mathsf{in})$. *The initial* $\mathcal{C}_{Q,T}$*-biautomaton is the functor* $\mathcal{A}_{init}(\mathcal{L}_{Q,T}): \mathcal{I}_{Q,T} \to \mathcal{C}$ *described in the following diagram*

$$\mathcal{L}(\mathsf{in}) \xrightarrow{\triangleright q_{init}} \coprod_{Q} \mathcal{L}(\mathsf{in}) \underset{\varepsilon_{init}}{\overset{a_{init}}{\rightrightarrows}} \coprod_{Q \cup QA} \mathcal{L}(\mathsf{in}) \xrightarrow{t\triangleleft_{init}} \mathcal{L}(\mathsf{out}),$$

where, explicitly:

- $\mathcal{A}_{init}(\mathcal{L}_{Q,T})(\mathsf{st}_1) = \coprod_{Q} \mathcal{L}(\mathsf{in})$ *and* $\mathcal{A}_{init}(\mathcal{L}_{Q,T})(\mathsf{st}_2) = \coprod_{Q \cup QA} \mathcal{L}(\mathsf{in})$;
- $\triangleright q_{init} := \mathcal{A}_{init}(\mathcal{L}_{Q,T})(\triangleright q)$ *is the coproduct injection* j_q *of* $\mathcal{L}(\mathsf{in})$ *into* $\coprod_{Q} \mathcal{L}(\mathsf{in})$;
- $\varepsilon_{init} := \mathcal{A}_{init}(\mathcal{L}_{Q,T})(\varepsilon)$ *is the canonical inclusion between the two coproducts;*
- $a_{init} := \mathcal{A}_{init}(\mathcal{L}_{Q,T})(a)$ *is obtained via the universal property as the coproduct over* $q \in Q$ *of the canonical injections* $j_{qa} \colon \mathcal{L}(\mathsf{in}) \to \coprod_{Q \cup QA} \mathcal{L}(\mathsf{in})$;
- $t\triangleleft_{init} := \mathcal{A}_{init}(\mathcal{L}_{Q,T})(t\triangleleft)$ *is obtained via the universal property as the coproduct over* $w \in Q \cup QA$ *of the morphisms* $\mathcal{L}(\triangleright wt\triangleleft) \colon \mathcal{L}(\mathsf{in}) \to \mathcal{L}(\mathsf{out})$.

Dually, the final $\mathcal{C}_{Q,T}$-biautomaton may be described as follows.

Lemma 4.1.5. *Assume* $\mathcal{C}$ *has all countable powers of* $\mathcal{L}(\mathsf{out})$. *The final* $\mathcal{C}_{Q,T}$-*biautomaton is the functor* $\mathcal{A}_{final}(\mathcal{L}_{Q,T}) \colon \mathcal{I}_{Q,T} \to \mathcal{C}$ *described in the following diagram*

$$\mathcal{L}(\mathsf{in}) \xrightarrow{\triangleright q_{final}} \prod_{T \cup AT} \mathcal{L}(\mathsf{out}) \underset{\varepsilon_{final}}{\overset{a_{final}}{\rightrightarrows}} \prod_{T} \mathcal{L}(\mathsf{out}) \xrightarrow{t\triangleleft_{final}} \mathcal{L}(\mathsf{out}),$$

where, explicitly:

- $\mathcal{A}_{final}(\mathcal{L}_{Q,T})(\mathsf{st}_1) = \prod_{T \cup AT} \mathcal{L}(\mathsf{out})$ *and* $\mathcal{A}_{init}(\mathcal{L}_{Q,T})(\mathsf{st}_2) = \prod_{T} \mathcal{L}(\mathsf{out})$;
- $\triangleright q_{final} := \mathcal{A}_{final}(\mathcal{L}_{Q,T})(\triangleright q)$ *is obtained via the universal property as the product over* $w \in T \cup AT$ *of the morphisms* $\mathcal{L}(\triangleright qw\triangleleft) \colon \mathcal{L}(\mathsf{in}) \to \mathcal{L}(\mathsf{out})$;
- $\varepsilon_{final} := \mathcal{A}_{final}(\mathcal{L}_{Q,T})(\varepsilon)$ *is the canonical restriction between the two products;*
- $a_{final} := \mathcal{A}_{final}(\mathcal{L}_{Q,T})(a)$ *is obtained via the universal property of* $\prod_{T} \mathcal{L}(\mathsf{out})$ *as the product over* $t \in T$ *of the canonical projections* $\pi_{at} \colon \prod_{T \cup AT} \mathcal{L}(\mathsf{out}) \to \mathcal{L}(\mathsf{out})$;
- $t\triangleleft_{final} := \mathcal{A}_{final}(\mathcal{L}_{Q,T})(t\triangleleft)$ *is the projection* $\pi_t \colon \prod_{T} \mathcal{L}(\mathsf{out}) \to \mathcal{L}(\mathsf{out})$.

Proof. It is easy to check directly the universal properties of the two objects.

Suppose there is a $\mathcal{C}_{Q,T}$-biautomaton $\mathcal{B}$:

$$\mathcal{L}(\mathsf{in}) \xrightarrow{\triangleright q} B_1 \underset{\varepsilon}{\overset{a}{\rightrightarrows}} B_2 \xrightarrow{t\triangleleft} \mathcal{L}(\mathsf{out}).$$

Let's define a morphism from $\mathcal{A}_{init}(\mathcal{L})$ to $\mathcal{B}$ as follows.

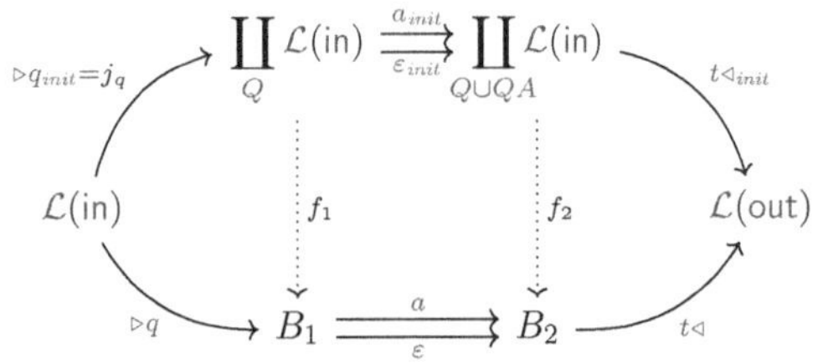

The morphism f_1 is defined using the universal property of $\coprod_Q \mathcal{L}(\mathsf{in})$ as the map $\coprod_{q \in Q} \mathcal{B}(\triangleright q)$. Similarly, f_2 is defined using the universal property of $\coprod_{Q \cup QA} \mathcal{L}(\mathsf{in})$ and the morphisms $\mathcal{B}(\varepsilon \circ \triangleright q)$ and $\mathcal{B}(a \circ \triangleright q)$.

Since f_1 and f_2 are defined using the universal property of the two coproducts, they must be unique.

In addition, this is a natural transformation: the triangle on the left commutes because of the definition of f_1; denoting by j_q the coproduct injections, the square in the middle commutes because $f_2 \circ a_{init} = a \circ f_1$ if and only if $f_2 \circ a_{init} \circ j_q = a \circ f_1 \circ j_q$ for all $q \in Q$, and $f_2 \circ \varepsilon_{init} = \varepsilon \circ f_1$ if and only if $f_2 \circ \varepsilon_{init} \circ j_q = \varepsilon \circ f_1 \circ j_q$ for all $q \in Q$; the triangle on the right commutes because $t\triangleleft \circ f_2 = t\triangleleft_{init}$ if and only if $t\triangleleft \circ f_2 \circ j_{\widetilde{q}} = t\triangleleft_{init} \circ j_{\widetilde{q}}$ for all $\widetilde{q} \in Q \cup QA$, $\mathcal{L}(\triangleright q a t \triangleleft) = \mathcal{L}(\triangleright q_{init} a_{init} t\triangleleft_{init})$ and $\mathcal{L}(\triangleright q t \triangleleft) = \mathcal{L}(\triangleright q_{init} t\triangleleft_{init})$.

The reasoning for the final object is perfectly dual. □

Combining Corollary 3.3.3 with Lemmas 3.3.4, 4.1.4 and 4.1.5, the minimal biautomaton $\mathsf{Min}(\mathcal{L}_{Q,T})$ in $\mathsf{Auto}(\mathcal{L}_{Q,T})$ may be obtained.

Theorem 4.1.6. *Assume that $\mathcal{C}$ is equipped with a factorization system $(\mathcal{E}, \mathcal{M})$ and has countable copowers of $\mathcal{L}(\mathsf{in})$ and countable powers of $\mathcal{L}(\mathsf{out})$. Then the minimal $\mathcal{C}_{Q,T}$-biautomaton $\mathsf{Min}(\mathcal{L}_{Q,T})$ is obtained as the unique up to isomorphism factorization of the unique morphism from $\mathcal{A}_{init}(\mathcal{L}_{Q,T})$ to $\mathcal{A}_{final}(\mathcal{L}_{Q,T})$.*

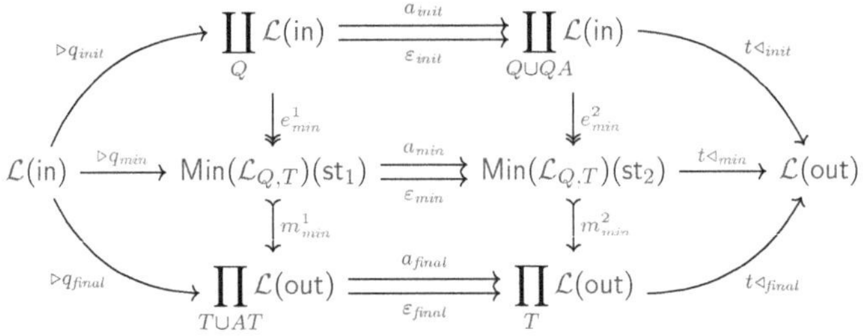

Notice that the arrows $\triangleright q_{min}$, a_{min}, ε_{min} and $t\triangleleft_{min}$ are obtained using the diagonal fill-in property of the factorization system, i.e. its functoriality (see Definition 3.1.1).

Let's see how this theorem instantiates in the case of deterministic automata.

Example 4.1.7. Assume the target language $\mathcal{L}$ is a $(\mathsf{Set}, 1, 2)$-language, so the learner wants to learn the minimal deterministic automaton accepting $\mathcal{L}$. For a given couple (Q, T), the minimal biautomaton is obtained as the following factorization.

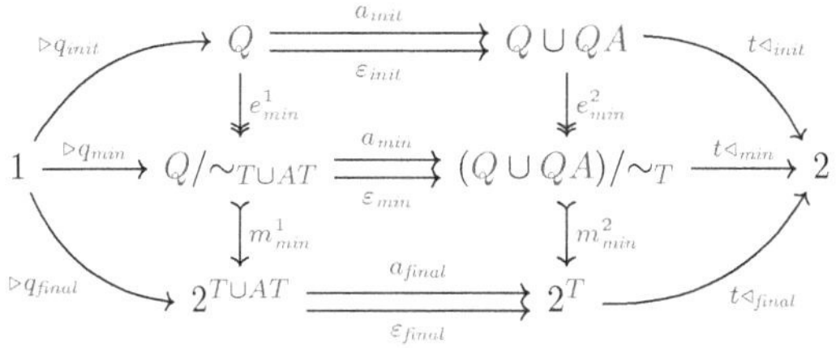

Hence, the first set of states of the minimal biautomaton is the set Q quotiented by the $T \cup AT$-approximation $\sim_{T\cup AT}$ of the Myhill-Nerode equivalence. The second set of states is the quotient of $Q \cup QA$ by $\sim_T$. These kinds of quotients are also needed in the classical Angluin's algorithm, when building the table corresponding to the couple (Q, T).

Let's now understand when the map ε_{min} is an isomorphism, that is, in this case, a bijection. It is easily verifiable that ε_{min} being a surjection is equivalent to the table in L^*-algorithm being closed, that is, for all $q \in Q$ and $a \in A$ there exists $q' \in Q$ such that $q' \sim_T qa$ (the property of $\mathcal{L}$-completeness in Definition 1.3.1). On the other hand, ε_{min} being an injection is equivalent to the consistency of the table from Angluin's L^*-algorithm, that is, if q and q' are such that $q \sim_T q'$, then $q \sim_{T\cup AT} q'$ (the property of $\mathcal{L}$-correctness in Definition 1.3.2).

If the table from Angluin's algorithm is generalized via the minimal biautomaton $\mathsf{Min}(\mathcal{L}_{Q,T})$, the above example suggests that the conditions that make possible the generation of a hypothesis automaton from a table can be stated at this abstract level by requiring the morphism ε_{min} be an isomorphism. In this way, $\mathsf{Min}(\mathcal{L})(\mathsf{st}_1)$ and $\mathsf{Min}(\mathcal{L})(\mathsf{st}_2)$ may be identified to obtain the state space of the hypothesis automaton.

Definition 4.1.8. If the map ε_{min} is an isomorphism, (Q, T) is said to be *$\mathcal{L}$-automatable*. The *hypothesis automaton* $\mathcal{H}(Q, T)$ associated to an $\mathcal{L}$-automatable couple (Q, T) is the $\mathcal{C}$-automaton with state space $\mathsf{Min}(\mathcal{L}_{Q,T})(\mathsf{st}_1)$ described on the generator arrows of $\mathcal{I}_{A^*}$ by

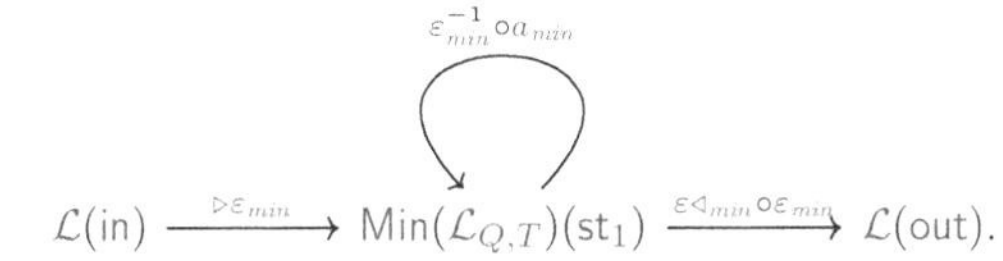
$\varepsilon^{-1}_{min} \circ a_{min}$
$\mathcal{L}(\mathsf{in})$
$\triangleright\varepsilon_{min}$
$\mathsf{Min}(\mathcal{L}_{Q,T})(\mathsf{st}_1)$
$\varepsilon\triangleleft_{min} \circ \varepsilon_{min}$
$\mathcal{L}(\mathsf{out})$.

The uniqueness up to isomorphism of the hypothesis automaton $\mathcal{H}(Q, T)$ is an easy consequence of the uniqueness up to isomorphism of the minimal biautomaton in $\mathsf{Auto}(\mathcal{L}_{Q,T})$.

It is important to remark that, when passing from a biautomaton to an automaton, the consistency with the language is preserved, in the sense of the lemma below.

Lemma 4.1.9. *Let (Q, T) be an $\mathcal{L}$-automatable couple and let $\mathcal{H}(Q, T)$ be its associated hypothesis automaton. Then the following diagram commutes:*

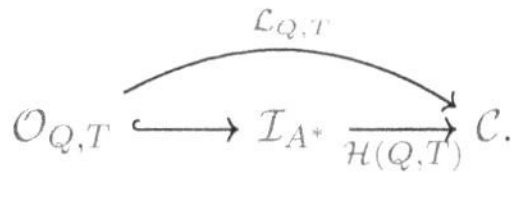

Proof. In order to prove the lemma, two equalities must hold for all $q \in Q$, $a \in A$ and $t \in T$:

- $\mathcal{H}(Q,T)(\triangleright qat\triangleleft) = \mathcal{L}(\triangleright qat\triangleleft)$;
- $\mathcal{H}(Q,T)(\triangleright qt\triangleleft) = \mathcal{L}(\triangleright qt\triangleleft)$.

Let's just prove the first item, as the second is similar. Consider a word $w \in A^*$, with $w = a^1 \dots a^n$ where $a^i \in A$. Upon seeing w as a morphism $w\colon \mathsf{st} \to \mathsf{st}$ in $\mathcal{I}_{A^*}$, $\mathcal{H}(Q,T)(w)$ is by definition the following composite.

$$\mathsf{Min}(\mathcal{L}_{Q,T})(\mathsf{st}_1) \xrightarrow{a^1_{min}} \mathsf{Min}(\mathcal{L}_{Q,T})(\mathsf{st}_2) \xrightarrow{\varepsilon^{-1}_{min}} \dots$$

$$\dots \xrightarrow{a^n_{min}} \mathsf{Min}(\mathcal{L}_{Q,T})(\mathsf{st}_2) \xrightarrow{\varepsilon^{-1}_{min}} \mathsf{Min}(\mathcal{L}_{Q,T})(\mathsf{st}_1)$$

Let's notice that:

- if $w \in Q$, then $\mathcal{H}(Q,T)(w) \circ \triangleright\varepsilon_{min} = \triangleright w_{min}$;
- if $w \in T$, then $\varepsilon\triangleleft_{min} \circ \varepsilon_{min} \circ \mathcal{H}(Q,T)(w) = w\triangleleft_{min} \circ \varepsilon_{min}$.

These statements follow easily by applying repeatedly the coherence diagrams from the definition of $\mathcal{I}_{Q,T}$ and using the prefix-closure of Q and the suffix-closure of T. To improve readability, let $\mathcal{H}$ stand for $\mathcal{H}(Q,T)$ in the following equalities, obtained by applying the previous equations:

$$\begin{aligned}
\mathcal{H}(Q,T)(\triangleright qat\triangleleft) &= (\varepsilon\triangleleft_{min} \circ \varepsilon_{min} \circ \mathcal{H}(t)) \circ \mathcal{H}(a) \circ \mathcal{H}(q) \circ \triangleright\varepsilon_{min} \\
&= (t\triangleleft_{min} \circ \varepsilon_{min}) \circ \mathcal{H}(a) \circ \mathcal{H}(q) \circ \triangleright\varepsilon_{min} \\
&= t\triangleleft_{min} \circ \varepsilon_{min} \circ (\varepsilon^{-1}_{min} \circ a_{min}) \circ \mathcal{H}(q) \circ \triangleright\varepsilon_{min} \\
&= t\triangleleft_{min} \circ a_{min} \circ (\mathcal{H}(q) \circ \triangleright\varepsilon_{min}) \\
&= t\triangleleft_{min} \circ a_{min} \circ \triangleright q_{min} \\
&= \mathsf{Min}(\mathcal{L}_{Q,T})(\triangleright qat\triangleleft) \\
&= \mathcal{L}(\triangleright qat\triangleleft).
\end{aligned}$$

Proving $\mathcal{H}(Q,T)(\triangleright qt\triangleleft) = \mathcal{L}(\triangleright qt\triangleleft)$ follows the same lines as above. □

4.2 The basic categorical learning algorithm

Now all the necessary ingredients to state the FunL*-algorithm have been presented. This algorithm takes as input a target language $\mathcal{L}$ and outputs its minimal automaton, provided some mild assumptions listed in Theorem 4.2.5 are satisfied.

Let's start by instantiating the couple (Q,T) by $(\{\varepsilon\},\{\varepsilon\})$. As long as this couple is not $\mathcal{L}$-automatable, further words are added to the subsets Q and T to force ε_{min} to become an isomorphism. Once this is achieved, a hypothesis automaton can be obtained. If this automaton does not recognize the target language, then the provided counterexample and its prefixes are added to Q, in order to let the learner progress in learning.

Definition 4.2.1. Let $\mathcal{A}$ be an automaton which is incorrect, that is, such that $\mathcal{A} \circ i \neq \mathcal{L}$, $\mathcal{L}$ being the target language. A word w is said to be a *counterexample* for $\mathcal{A}$ to accept $\mathcal{L}$ if $\mathcal{A} \circ i(\triangleright w \triangleleft) \neq \mathcal{L}(\triangleright w \triangleleft)$.

In other words, a counterexample witnesses the incorrectness of a certain automaton proposed by the learner.

While the role played by equivalence queries is self-evident, notice that evaluation queries are necessary in order to build up the category $\mathsf{Auto}(\mathcal{L}_{Q,T})$ and analyse its minimal automaton.

input : minimally adequate teacher of the target language $\mathcal{L}$
output: $\mathsf{Min}(\mathcal{L})$
$Q := T := \{\varepsilon\}$
repeat
  while (Q, T) *is not* $\mathcal{L}$*-automatable* **do**
    if $\varepsilon_{min} \notin \mathcal{E}$ **then**
      add QA to Q
    end
    if $\varepsilon_{min} \notin \mathcal{M}$ **then**
      add AT to T
    end
  end
  ask an equivalence query for the hypothesis automaton $\mathcal{H}(Q, T)$
  if *the answer is no* **then**
    add the provided counterexample and all its prefixes to Q
  end
until *the answer is yes*;
return $\mathcal{H}(Q, T)$

Algorithm 4.2.2. The basic FunL**-algorithm*

In order for this generic algorithm to work, several mild assumptions on the output category $\mathcal{C}$ and on the target language are needed. First, in order to compute the hypothesis automaton, the existence of the minimal automaton in the category $\mathsf{Auto}(\mathcal{L}_{Q,T})$ is needed. For this reason, the hypothesis of Theorem 4.1.6 are assumed, pertaining to the existence of certain powers, certain copowers and a factorization system. Furthermore, in order to ensure the termination of the algorithm, a noetherianity condition is required on the language $\mathcal{L}$, akin to the regularity of the language in the L^*-algorithm. This notion, also used in [20], can be understood as a finiteness assumption as shown in Example 4.2.4.

Definition 4.2.3. An object X of $\mathcal{C}$ is called $(\mathcal{E}, \mathcal{M})$*-noetherian* when the following conditions hold.

- There does not exist an infinite co-chain of $\mathcal{E}$-quotients of X as in the left commutative diagram below and such that the arrows $e_1, e_2 \ldots \in \mathcal{E}$ are not isomorphisms.
- There does not exist an infinite chain of $\mathcal{M}$-subobjects of X as in the right commutative diagram below and such that the arrows $m_1, m_2 \ldots \in \mathcal{M}$ are not isomorphisms.

Example 4.2.4. It is easy to see that in the category Set an object X is (Surjections, Injections)-noetherian if and only if it is finite in the usual sense.

To guarantee the termination of the algorithm, the $(\mathcal{E}, \mathcal{M})$-noetherianity of the state space of the minimal automaton of the target language is required: this is a natural condition, generalizing the regularity of the target language in the L^*-algorithm.

Remark that, if $(\mathcal{E}, \mathcal{M})$-noetherian objects are closed under $\mathcal{E}$-quotients and $\mathcal{M}$-subobjects, as it is the case in all the given instantiations, this hypothesis could be replaced by assuming the existence of an automaton with $(\mathcal{E}, \mathcal{M})$-noetherian state space which accepts the target language.

Theorem 4.2.5. *Let's consider a target language $\mathcal{L}\colon \mathcal{O}_{A^*} \to \mathcal{C}$ such that:*

- *the output category $\mathcal{C}$ is endowed with a factorization system $(\mathcal{E}, \mathcal{M})$;*
- *$\mathcal{C}$ has all countable copowers of $\mathcal{L}(\mathsf{in})$ and all countable powers of $\mathcal{L}(\mathsf{out})$;*
- *the state space $\mathsf{Min}(\mathcal{L})(\mathsf{st})$ of the minimal automaton for $\mathcal{L}$ is $(\mathcal{E}, \mathcal{M})$-noetherian.*

Then the FunL* *-algorithm terminates, eventually producing the minimal automaton $\mathsf{Min}(\mathcal{L})$ accepting the target language.*

The proof of this theorem relies on a careful analysis of the factorizations

$$\textstyle\coprod_Q \mathcal{L}(\mathsf{in}) \twoheadrightarrow \Im_{Q,T} \rightarrowtail \prod_T \mathcal{L}(\mathsf{out})$$

of the canonical maps $\coprod_Q \mathcal{L}(\mathsf{in}) \to \prod_T \mathcal{L}(\mathsf{out})$ obtained by taking the coproduct over $q \in Q$ of the product over $t \in T$ of $\mathcal{L}(\triangleright qt \triangleleft)$.

The fact that the while loop terminates is proved in Proposition 4.2.12; in Lemma 4.2.13 it is shown that only finitely many counterexamples can be added, hence the algorithm terminates; finally, the fact that the outcome automaton is minimal is shown in Lemma 4.2.15.

Definition 4.2.6. For all couples (Q, T), the language $\mathcal{L}$ induces a canonical map

$$\coprod_{q\in Q}\prod_{t\in T} \mathcal{L}(\triangleright qt \triangleleft)\colon \coprod_Q \mathcal{L}(\mathsf{in}) \to \prod_T \mathcal{L}(\mathsf{out}),$$

obtained using the universal properties of the coproduct, respectively of the product. $\Im_{Q,T}(\mathcal{L})$ (or simply $\Im_{Q,T}$) is defined to be the factorization of this map

$$\textstyle\coprod_Q \mathcal{L}(\mathsf{in}) \twoheadrightarrow \Im_{Q,T} \rightarrowtail \prod_T \mathcal{L}(\mathsf{out}).$$

The objects $\Im_{Q,T}$ play a crucial role in the proof of termination of the FunL*-algorithm. First notice that, when $Q = T = A^*$, then $\Im_{A^*,A^*}$ is nothing else but the state space of the minimal automaton $\mathsf{Min}(\mathcal{L})$, as computed in Theorem 3.3.9. More generally, for an arbitrary (Q, T), objects of the form $\Im_{Q,T}$ are featured in the minimal $\mathcal{C}_{Q,T}$-biautomaton $\mathsf{Min}(\mathcal{L}_{Q,T})$, whose computation from Theorem 4.1.6 is recalled below.

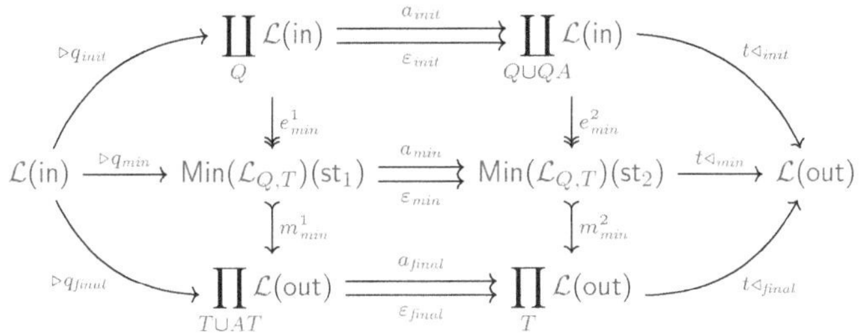

Indeed, a careful analysis of the situation described in the above diagram reveals that when computing the unique map from $\mathcal{A}_{init}(\mathcal{L}_{Q,T})$ to $\mathcal{A}_{final}(\mathcal{L}_{Q,T})$ one obtains that:

- the unique map $\mathcal{A}_{init}(\mathcal{L}_{Q,T})(\mathsf{st}_1) \to \mathcal{A}_{final}(\mathcal{L}_{Q,T})(\mathsf{st}_1)$ is the canonical map

$$\coprod_{q\in Q} \prod_{t\in T\cup AT} \mathcal{L}(\triangleright qt\triangleleft)\colon \coprod_{Q} \mathcal{L}(\mathsf{in}) \to \prod_{T\cup AT} \mathcal{L}(\mathsf{out})\,;$$

- the unique map $\mathcal{A}_{init}(\mathcal{L}_{Q,T})(\mathsf{st}_2) \to \mathcal{A}_{final}(\mathcal{L}_{Q,T})(\mathsf{st}_2)$ is the canonical map

$$\coprod_{q\in Q\cup QA} \prod_{t\in T} \mathcal{L}(\triangleright qt\triangleleft)\colon \coprod_{Q\cup QA} \mathcal{L}(\mathsf{in}) \to \prod_{T} \mathcal{L}(\mathsf{out})\,;$$

- the composite map $m^2_{min} \circ \varepsilon_{min} \circ e^1_{min}$ is the canonical map

$$\coprod_{q\in Q} \prod_{t\in T} \mathcal{L}(\triangleright qt\triangleleft)\colon \coprod_{Q} \mathcal{L}(\mathsf{in}) \to \prod_{T} \mathcal{L}(\mathsf{out})\,.$$

Therefore the following lemma may be obtained.

Lemma 4.2.7. *The states of the minimal $\mathcal{C}_{Q,T}$-biautomaton* $\mathsf{Min}(\mathcal{L}_{Q,T})$ *are $\Im_{Q,T\cup AT}$ and, respectively, $\Im_{Q\cup QA,T}$.*

Proof. See Definition 4.2.6. □

The next lemma lists some simple, yet very useful properties of the objects $\Im_{Q,T}$.

Lemma 4.2.8. *Let's assume Q, Q', T, T' are subsets of A^* such that $Q \subseteq Q'$ and $T \subseteq T'$. The following properties hold.*

1. *There exists a unique canonical $\mathcal{M}$-morphism $\Im_{Q,T} \rightarrowtail \Im_{Q',T}$ such that the following diagram commutes, in which can denotes the canonical morphism between the two coproducts.*

$$\begin{array}{ccccc}
\coprod_Q \mathcal{L}(\mathsf{in}) & \twoheadrightarrow & \Im_{Q,T} & \rightarrowtail & \prod_T \mathcal{L}(\mathsf{out}) \\
\downarrow{\scriptstyle can} & & \vdots & & \| \\
\coprod_{Q'} \mathcal{L}(\mathsf{in}) & \twoheadrightarrow & \Im_{Q',T} & \rightarrowtail & \prod_T \mathcal{L}(\mathsf{out})
\end{array}$$

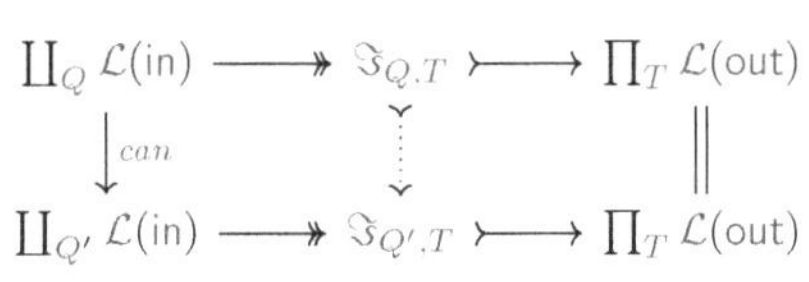

2. *There exists a unique canonical $\mathcal{E}$-morphism* $\Im_{Q,T'} \twoheadrightarrow \Im_{Q,T}$ *such that the following diagram commutes, in which* can *denotes the canonical morphism between the two products.*

$$\begin{array}{ccccc}
\coprod_Q \mathcal{L}(\mathsf{in}) & \twoheadrightarrow & \Im_{Q,T'} & \rightarrowtail & \prod_{T'} \mathcal{L}(\mathsf{out}) \\
\| & & \vdots\!\downarrow & & \downarrow{\scriptstyle can} \\
\coprod_Q \mathcal{L}(\mathsf{in}) & \twoheadrightarrow & \Im_{Q,T} & \rightarrowtail & \prod_{T} \mathcal{L}(\mathsf{out})
\end{array}$$

3. *For these canonical morphisms, the following diagram commutes:*

$$\begin{array}{ccc}
\Im_{Q,T'} & \rightarrowtail & \Im_{Q',T'} \\
\downarrow & & \downarrow \\
\Im_{Q,T} & \rightarrowtail & \Im_{Q',T}.
\end{array}$$

4. *Furthermore, if* $\Im_{Q,T'} \rightarrowtail \Im_{Q',T'}$ *is an isomorphism, then so is*

   $\Im_{Q,T} \rightarrowtail \Im_{Q',T}$.

5. *And dually, if* $\Im_{Q',T'} \twoheadrightarrow \Im_{Q',T}$ *is an isomorphism, then so is*

   $\Im_{Q,T'} \twoheadrightarrow \Im_{Q,T}$.

6. *The canonical morphisms compose well, that is, for $Q' \subseteq Q''$ and $T' \subseteq T''$, the following diagrams commute.*

Proof. 1. The existence and uniqueness of the morphism follows from the functoriality of the factorization system $(\mathcal{E}, \mathcal{M})$. The fact that it is in $\mathcal{M}$ follows from the left cancellation property of $\mathcal{M}$, see Lemma 3.1.5.

2. The proof is dual to that of the previous item.

3. By virtue of the functoriality of the factorization system, there exists a unique (canonical) morphism $\Im_{Q,T'} \longrightarrow \Im_{Q',T}$ such that the following diagram commutes, in which the vertical arrows denote the canonical morphisms between the two coproducts, respectively between the two products.

$$\begin{array}{ccccc}
\coprod_Q \mathcal{L}(\mathsf{in}) & \twoheadrightarrow & \Im_{Q,T'} & \rightarrowtail & \prod_{T'} \mathcal{L}(\mathsf{out}) \\
\downarrow{\scriptstyle can} & & \vdots\!\downarrow{\scriptstyle \exists!} & & \downarrow{\scriptstyle can} \\
\coprod_{Q'} \mathcal{L}(\mathsf{in}) & \twoheadrightarrow & \Im_{Q',T} & \rightarrowtail & \prod_{T} \mathcal{L}(\mathsf{out})
\end{array}$$

The commutativity of the diagram follows since both the arrows $\Im_{Q,T'} \rightarrowtail \Im_{Q',T'} \twoheadrightarrow \Im_{Q',T}$ and $\Im_{Q,T'} \twoheadrightarrow \Im_{Q,T} \rightarrowtail \Im_{Q',T}$ make the above diagram commute.

4. Assume $\Im_{Q,T'} \rightarrowtail \Im_{Q',T'}$ is an isomorphism. Then the canonical morphism

$$\Im_{Q,T'} \longrightarrow \Im_{Q',T}$$

is in $\mathcal{E}$. Using the right cancellation property of $\mathcal{E}$, one gets that the canonical morphism $\Im_{Q,T} \rightarrowtail \Im_{Q',T}$ is in $\mathcal{E}$. Since it is already in $\mathcal{M}$, it must be in $\mathcal{E} \cap \mathcal{M}$, hence it is an isomorphism.

5. The proof is dual to that of the previous item.

6. The proof is very similar to that of item 3 and relies on the uniqueness of the canonical morphisms.

□

Using Lemma 4.2.7 together with items 1 and 2 of Lemma 4.2.8, one obtains that $\Im_{Q,T}$ is a $(\mathcal{E}, \mathcal{M})$-factorization of the morphism ε_{min}. To underline the dependence of ε_{min} on Q and T, hereafter this map will be denoted by $\varepsilon_{min}^{Q,T}$.

Lemma 4.2.9. *The morphism* $\varepsilon_{min}^{Q,T} = \mathsf{Min}(\mathcal{L}_{Q,T})(\varepsilon)$ *is the composite of the canonical morphisms* $\Im_{Q,T\cup AT} \twoheadrightarrow \Im_{Q,T} \rightarrowtail \Im_{Q\cup QA,T}$. *Consequently:*

- *if* $\varepsilon_{min}^{Q,T} \notin \mathcal{E}$, *then* $\Im_{Q,T} \rightarrowtail \Im_{Q\cup QA,T}$ *is not an isomorphism;*
- *if* $\varepsilon_{min}^{Q,T} \notin \mathcal{M}$, *then* $\Im_{Q,T\cup AT} \twoheadrightarrow \Im_{Q,T}$ *is not an isomorphism.*

Proof. In a diagram, one has the following situation:

$$\begin{array}{ccccc}
\coprod_Q \mathcal{L}(\mathsf{in}) & & \xrightarrow{\quad \varepsilon_{init} \quad} & & \coprod_{Q\cup QA} \mathcal{L}(\mathsf{in}) \\
\downarrow & & & & \downarrow \\
\Im_{Q,T\cup AT} & \twoheadrightarrow & \Im_{Q,T} & \rightarrowtail & \Im_{Q\cup QA,T} \\
\downarrow & & & & \downarrow \\
\prod_{T\cup AT} \mathcal{L}(\mathsf{out}) & & \xrightarrow[\quad \varepsilon_{final} \quad]{} & & \prod_T \mathcal{L}(\mathsf{out}).
\end{array}$$

The second part of the lemma is immediate, since $\mathcal{E}$ and $\mathcal{M}$ contain the isomorphisms and are closed under composition. □

Before proving the termination of the while cycle, two more results are required: they use the $(\mathcal{E}, \mathcal{M})$-noetherianity of the state space of the minimal automaton $\mathsf{Min}(\mathcal{L})$.

Lemma 4.2.10. *The following hold.*

1. *There does not exist an infinite sequence of subsets* $(T_n)_n$ *with* $T_n \subseteq T_{n+1}$ *and such that the canonical morphisms below are not isomorphisms:*

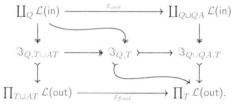

$$\mathfrak{I}_{A^*,T_1} \twoheadleftarrow \mathfrak{I}_{A^*,T_2} \twoheadleftarrow \mathfrak{I}_{A^*,T_3} \twoheadleftarrow \cdots$$

2. *Dually, there does not exist an infinite sequence of subsets $(Q_n)_n$ with $Q_n \subseteq Q_{n+1}$ and such that the canonical morphisms below are not isomorphisms:*

$$\mathfrak{I}_{Q_1,A^*} \rightarrowtail \mathfrak{I}_{Q_2,A^*} \rightarrowtail \mathfrak{I}_{Q_3,A^*} \rightarrowtail \cdots$$

Proof. Notice that, by item 6 of Lemma 4.2.8, the following diagram of canonical $\mathcal{E}$-quotients commutes.

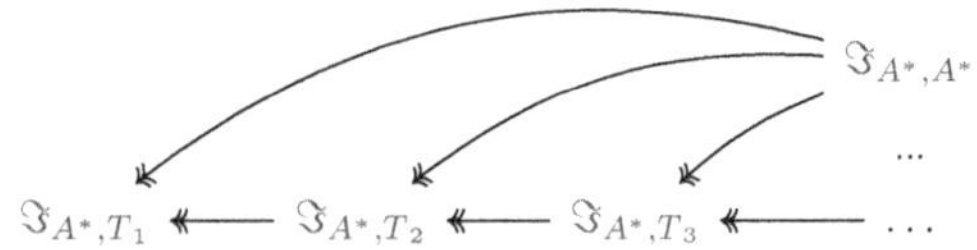

One concludes that such a sequence cannot exist upon recalling that $\mathfrak{I}_{A^*,A^*}$ is isomorphic to the state space of the minimal automaton and hence it is $(\mathcal{E},\mathcal{M})$-noetherian. By the first property from Definition 4.2.3, such a sequence cannot exist.

The proof for the second part is dual, as now one has an infinite sequence of $\mathcal{M}$-subobjects of $\mathfrak{I}_{A^*,A^*}$ and one can use the second property from Definition 4.2.3. □

In proving the termination of the while loop, one can consider sequences of couples $(Q_i, T_i)_{i\geq 1}$, which can be added either because $\varepsilon_{min}^{Q_i,T_i}$ is not in $\mathcal{E}$ or because it is not in $\mathcal{M}$, obtaining an $\mathcal{E}$-quotient $\mathfrak{I}_{Q_i,T_i} \overset{e_i}{\twoheadleftarrow} \mathfrak{I}_{Q_{i+1},T_{i+1}}$ or a $\mathcal{M}$-subobject $\mathfrak{I}_{Q_i,T_i} \overset{m_i}{\rightarrowtail} \mathfrak{I}_{Q_{i+1},T_{i+1}}$.

For this reason, the next lemma will prove helpful.

Lemma 4.2.11. *Consider a possibly infinite sequence of couples $(Q_i, T_i)_{i\geq 1}$ related by morphisms $(f_i)_{i\geq 1}$ such that for all i either*

- *$Q_i \subseteq Q_{i+1}$, $T_i = T_{i+1}$ and f_i is the canonical $\mathfrak{I}_{Q_i,T_i} \overset{m_i}{\rightarrowtail} \mathfrak{I}_{Q_{i+1},T_{i+1}}$, or*
- *$Q_{i+1} = Q_i$, $T_i \subseteq T_{i+1}$ and f_i is the canonical $\mathfrak{I}_{Q_i,T_i} \overset{e_i}{\twoheadleftarrow} \mathfrak{I}_{Q_{i+1},T_{i+1}}$.*

Then there can only be finitely many morphisms in $(f_i)_{i\geq 1}$ not being isomorphisms.

Proof. Using items 3 and 6 of Lemma 4.2.8 for each index i, one gets that the morphism f_i is at the bottom of exactly one of the following diagrams. Notice, however, that for the diagram on the right, since one is in the case when $Q_i = Q_{i+1}$, the canonical morphism at the top is actually the identity.

$$\begin{array}{ccc} \mathfrak{I}_{Q_i,A^*} & \overset{\overline{m_i}}{\rightarrowtail} & \mathfrak{I}_{Q_{i+1},A^*} \\ \downarrow & & \downarrow \\ \mathfrak{I}_{Q_i,T_i} & \underset{m_i}{\rightarrowtail} & \mathfrak{I}_{Q_{i+1},T_{i+1}} \end{array} \qquad \begin{array}{ccc} \mathfrak{I}_{Q_i,A^*} & = & \mathfrak{I}_{Q_{i+1},A^*} \\ \downarrow & & \downarrow \\ \mathfrak{I}_{Q_i,T_i} & \underset{e_i}{\twoheadleftarrow} & \mathfrak{I}_{Q_{i+1},T_{i+1}} \end{array}$$

Therefore, one obtains a sequence

$$\Im_{Q_1,A^*} \xrightarrow{\overline{f_1}} \Im_{Q_2,A^*} \xrightarrow{\overline{f_2}} \Im_{Q_3,A^*} \qquad \cdots$$

where each $\overline{f_i}$ is either the morphism $\overline{m_i}$ from the left diagram above or the identity in the second case. Notice additionally that, using item 4 of Lemma 4.2.8, if m_i is not an isomorphism, then $\overline{m_i}$ is not either: otherwise, one would get that m_i is an isomorphism, contradicting the hypothesis.

By Lemma 4.2.10, the sequence $(\overline{f_i})_i$ can contain only finitely many morphisms of the form $\overline{m_i}$ not being isomorphisms.

In a completely dual manner, one can prove that only for finitely many indexes i the morphisms f_i are of the form e_i not being isomorphisms. Indeed, in this case one would exhibit a sequence of the form

$$\Im_{A^*,T_1} \xleftarrow[\widetilde{f_1}]{} \Im_{A^*,T_2} \xleftarrow[\widetilde{f_2}]{} \Im_{A^*,T_3} \qquad \cdots$$

where each $\widetilde{f_i}$ is either the identity or a canonical morphism $\widetilde{e_i}$, i.e. a lifting of e_i, which by virtue of item 5 of Lemma 4.2.8 cannot be an isomorphism if e_i is not an isomorphism. One concludes just as above using Lemma 4.2.10.

Since only finitely many f_is are of the form m_i not being isomorphisms and only finitely many of them are of the form e_i not being isomorphisms, the conclusion is that there can only be finitely many morphisms not being isomorphisms in the whole sequence. □

The termination of the while cycle may now be proved.

Proposition 4.2.12. *The while loop on line 3 of Algorithm 4.2.2 terminates.*

Proof. Consider a possibly infinite sequence $(Q_i, T_i)_{i\geq 1}$ obtained via a run of the while loop. Notice that for each i the couple (Q_{i+1}, T_{i+1}) was obtained from (Q_i, T_i) either because

a) $\varepsilon_{min}^{Q_i,T_i} \notin \mathcal{E}$, or

b) $\varepsilon_{min}^{Q_i,T_i} \notin \mathcal{M}$.

Therefore, in the respective cases, one has either

a) $Q_{i+1} = Q_i \cup Q_i A$ and $T_{i+1} = T_i$, or

b) $Q_{i+1} = Q_i$ and $T_{i+1} = T_i \cup AT_i$.

Let f_i denote exactly one of the following canonical morphisms, depending on the respective case:

a) $\Im_{Q_i,T_i} \xrightarrow{m_i} \Im_{Q_{i+1},T_{i+1}}$, or

b) $\Im_{Q_i,T_i} \xleftarrow[e_i]{} \Im_{Q_{i+1},T_{i+1}}$.

Notice that by Lemma 4.2.9 none of the morphisms f_i is an isomorphism: as a consequence, Lemma 4.2.11 may be applied to conclude that the sequence $(Q_i, T_i)_{i\geq 1}$ is finite. □

Lemma 4.2.13. *Only a finite number of counterexamples with their prefixes can be added to Q.*

Proof. The situation is as follows:

- the learner asks an equivalence query for an $\mathcal{L}$-automatable couple (Q, T);
- the teacher answers the query negatively and provides a counterexample $w \in A^*$;
- the learner adds the counterexample and all its prefixes to Q, then he runs the while cycle and obtains a new $\mathcal{L}$-automatable couple (Q', T'), with w and its prefixes still belonging to Q'.

The aim is to show that the complexity of the produced hypothesis automata strictly increases every time a counterexample and its prefixes are added to Q.

As (Q, T) and (Q', T') are automatable, the fundamental commuting diagrams of the categories $\text{Auto}(\mathcal{L}_{Q,T})$ and $\text{Auto}(\mathcal{L}_{Q',T'})$ may be supposed to be as follows.

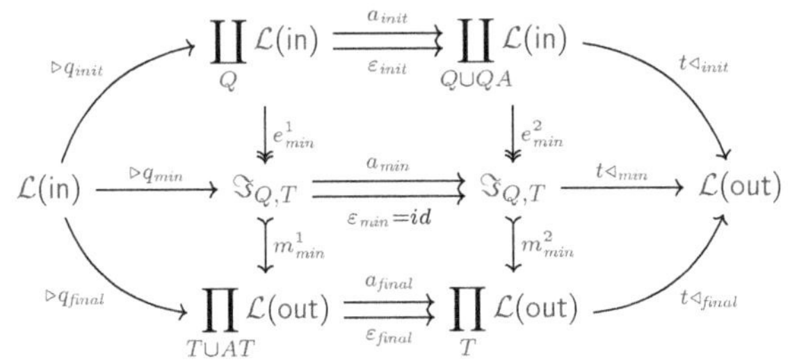

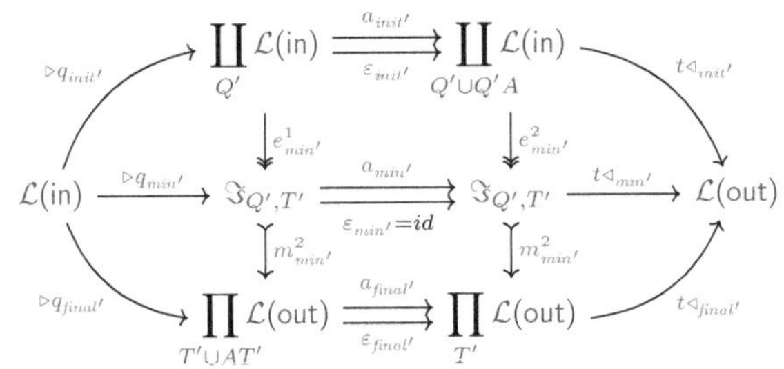

Let's show that the canonical arrows between the factorizations $\Im_{Q,T}$ and $\Im_{Q',T'}$ cannot be all isomorphisms: by contradiction, suppose they are.

$$\begin{array}{ccc} \Im_{Q,T'} & \xrightarrow{\cong} & \Im_{Q',T'} \\ {\scriptstyle \mathbb{R}}\downarrow & & {\scriptstyle \mathbb{R}}\downarrow \\ \Im_{Q,T} & \xrightarrow{\cong} & \Im_{Q',T} \end{array}$$

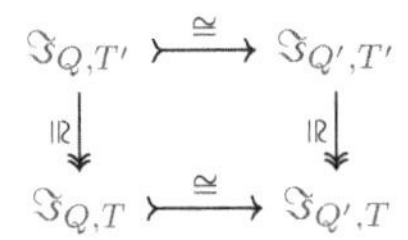

Let's consider the minimal biautomaton in $\text{Auto}(\mathcal{L}_{Q',T'})$ as a biautomaton in $\text{Auto}(\mathcal{L}_{Q,T})$, that is, without the arrows $\triangleright q_{min'}$ for $q \in Q' \setminus Q$ and the ones $t \triangleleft_{min'}$ for $t \in T' \setminus T$.

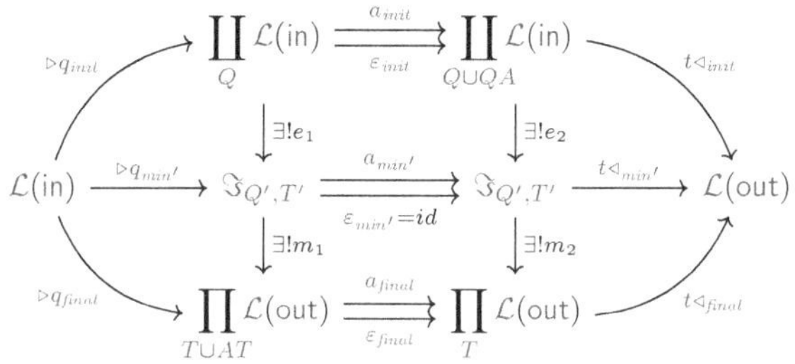

It turns out that $e_1, e_2 \in \mathcal{E}$ and $m_1, m_2 \in \mathcal{M}$: just the first fact may be proved, the second one being analogous. To underline the involved sets, let's use $res_{T',T}$ and $inc_{Q,Q'}$ to denote respectively the canonical restriction between products and the canonical inclusion between coproducts.

- It is easy to check that e_1 must be equal to $e^1_{min'} \circ inc_{Q,Q'}$ for the universal property of the coproduct; as a consequence of one of the diagrams related to the factorizations supposed to be isomorphic, one gets that $e_1 \in \mathcal{E}$.

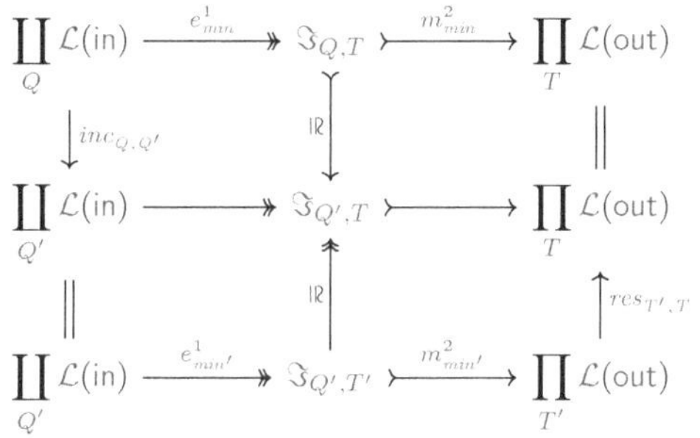

- It is easy to check that e_2 must be equal to $e^2_{min'} \circ inc_{Q\cup QA,Q'\cup Q'A}$ for the universal property of the coproduct, too; the fact that it belongs to $\mathcal{E}$ comes from the following commuting diagram.

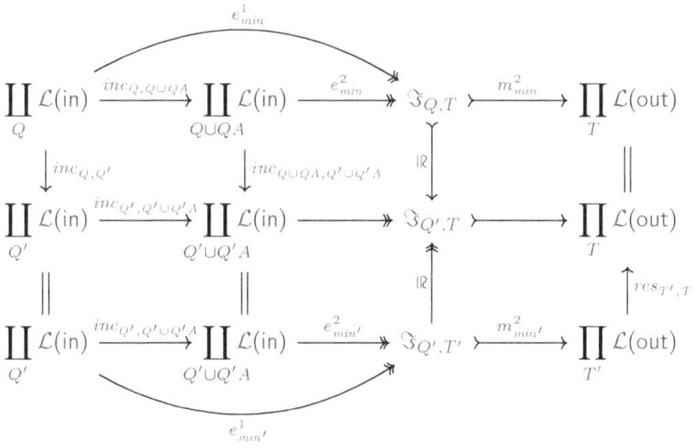

So, the two minimal objects are isomorphic as biautomata in $\mathsf{Auto}(\mathcal{L}_{Q,T})$; as a consequence, the associated hypothesis automata $\mathcal{H}(Q,T)$ and $\mathcal{H}(Q',T')$ are isomorphic, too: therefore, they accept the same language, leading to a contradiction.

In fact, the two hypothesis automata associated to the couples (Q,T) and (Q',T') differ on the counterexample: $\mathcal{H}(Q,T)$ is such that $\mathcal{H}(Q,T) \circ i(\triangleright w \triangleleft) \neq \mathcal{L}(\triangleright w \triangleleft)$, whereas $\mathcal{H}(Q',T')$ is such that $\mathcal{H}(Q',T') \circ i(\triangleright w \triangleleft) = \mathcal{L}(\triangleright w \triangleleft)$, w being the counterexample whose prefixes are included in Q' (see Lemma 4.1.9).

This means that every time a counterexample and its prefixes are added to Q, one gets a couple of arrows going from the factorization related to the previous hypothesis automaton to the factorization of the following one such that at least one of them is not an isomorphism.

$$\mathfrak{I}_{Q,T} \rightarrowtail \mathfrak{I}_{Q',T} \twoheadleftarrow \mathfrak{I}_{Q',T'}$$

Lemma 4.2.11 states that such a sequence cannot be infinite, so the number of counterexamples with their prefixes that can be added is finite. □

It remains to prove that the produced automaton is minimal: the following lemma will be used.

Lemma 4.2.14. *Let $\mathcal{C}$ be a category endowed with an initial object I, a final object F and a factorization system $(\mathcal{E},\mathcal{M})$.*

Let K be an $(\mathcal{E},\mathcal{M})$-noetherian object dividing the $(\mathcal{E},\mathcal{M})$-minimal object Min.

K is isomorphic to Min.

Proof. It is well known that the minimal object Min in such a category is the factorization of the only arrow from the initial to the final object and, as a consequence, is defined up to isomorphism (see Lemma 3.3.2).

Let's suppose that an $(\mathcal{E},\mathcal{M})$-noetherian object K divides Min, so there exists an object $\widetilde{K}$ such that K is a quotient of $\widetilde{K}$, which is a subobject of Min.

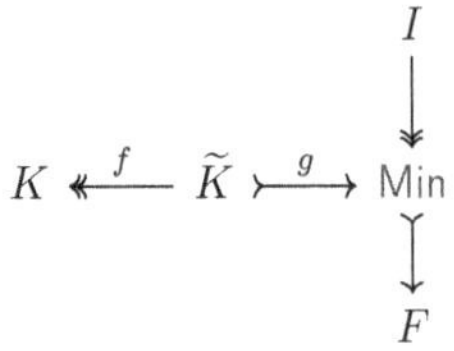

Consider the only arrow from K to F together with its factorization K', f' being the morphism in $\mathcal{E}$ of the $(\mathcal{E},\mathcal{M})$-factorization of such an arrow.

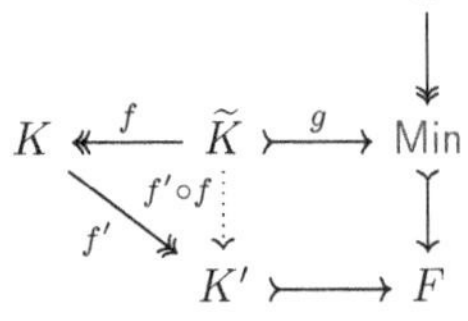

$f' \circ f$ clearly belongs to $\mathcal{E}$, but also belongs to $\mathcal{M}$, as the square on the right commutes (F is a final object): as a consequence, $f' \circ f$ is an isomorphism, hence it may be supposed that $K' = \widetilde{K}$ and $f' \circ f = id_{\widetilde{K}}$.

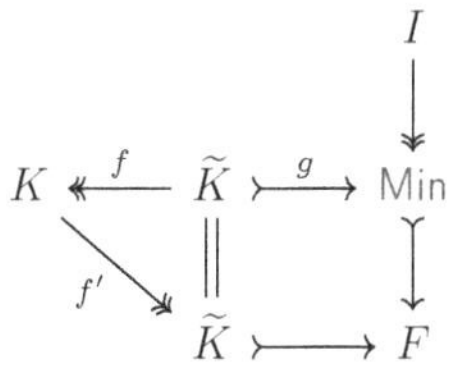

Now observe that the following diagram commutes.

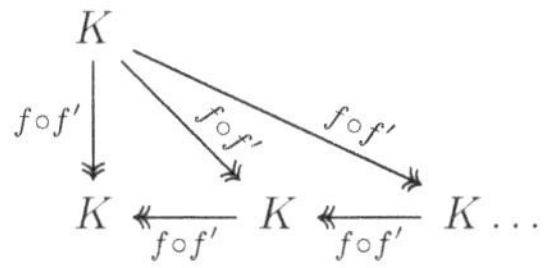

By virtue of the $(\mathcal{E}, \mathcal{M})$-noetherianity of K, $f \circ f'$ must be an isomorphism; in these conditions, it is easy to check that $f \circ f' = id_K$, so f is an isomorphism.

An analogous reasoning with arrows in $\mathcal{M}$ shows that g is an isomorphism too, concluding the proof. □

Lemma 4.2.15. *The automaton produced by Algorithm 4.2.2 is the minimal one* $\mathsf{Min}(\mathcal{L})$.

Proof. Let (Q, T) be the last couple produced by the algorithm.

In $\mathsf{Auto}(\mathcal{L})$, the minimal $\mathsf{Min}(\mathcal{L})$ divides any other object, the hypothesis automaton $\mathcal{H}(Q, T)$ too; so, $\mathsf{Min}(\mathcal{L})$ is a quotient of a certain automaton $\mathcal{A}$ being subobject of $\mathcal{H}(Q, T)$.

Now, one can consider all these automata as particular biautomata, taking their precomposition with the functor i^* (see Lemma 4.1.2).

In $\mathsf{Auto}(\mathcal{L}_{Q,T})$, it is easy to check that $\mathsf{Min}(\mathcal{L}) \circ i^*$ is $(\mathcal{E}, \mathcal{M})$-noetherian and divides $\mathcal{H}(Q, T) \circ i^*$ by means of $\mathcal{A} \circ i^*$ itself.

In addition, $\mathcal{H}(Q, T) \circ i^*$ is clearly the minimal biautomaton.

Lemma 4.2.14 guarantees that $\mathcal{H}(Q, T) \circ i^*$ and $\mathsf{Min}(\mathcal{L}) \circ i^*$ are isomorphic, so they are also isomorphic as hypothesis automata, that is, as objects in $\mathsf{Auto}(\mathcal{L})$. □

All together, these results prove the termination and correctness of the FunL*-algorithm as stated in Theorem 4.2.5.

Proof of Theorem 4.2.5. Proposition 4.2.12 guarantees that each while loop the learner performs cannot go on forever and terminates after a finite number of iterations.

After exiting each while loop, the algorithm performs an equivalence query: if the answer is negative, a counterexample and its prefixes are added to Q, but this operation may happen just a finite number of times, by virtue of Proposition 4.2.13.

Therefore, the algorithm must terminate.

The only possible way the algorithm can terminate is by asking an equivalence query returning a positive answer: this means that the hypothesis automaton associated to the latest couple accepts the target language.

The fact that the outcome automaton is minimal is shown in Lemma 4.2.15. □

4.3 The optimized categorical learning algorithm

Every time the while cycle runs, the basic FunL*-algorithm adds either all words QA to Q or all words AT to T: this is not strictly necessary. Let's show that it is sufficient to add just one properly chosen single word $qa \in QA$ or $at \in AT$, preserving the correctness of the algorithm. The canonical inclusion $\coprod_Q \mathcal{L}(\mathsf{in}) \to \coprod_{Q\cup\{qa\}} \mathcal{L}(\mathsf{in})$ induces a canonical morphism between the factorizations $\Im_{Q,T} \rightarrowtail \Im_{Q\cup\{qa\},T}$. Similarly, the canonical restriction $\prod_{T\cup\{at\}} \mathcal{L}(\mathsf{out}) \to \prod_T \mathcal{L}(\mathsf{out})$ induces a canonical morphism between the factorizations $\Im_{Q,T} \twoheadleftarrow \Im_{Q,T\cup\{at\}}$. These two morphisms will be featured in the optimized FunL*-algorithm.

Theorem 4.3.1. *Algorithm 4.2.2 can be optimized by replacing lines 5 and 8 respectively by:*

- add to Q a $qa \in QA$ s.t. $\Im_{Q,T} \rightarrowtail \Im_{Q\cup\{qa\},T}$ is not an isomorphism;
- add to T an $at \in AT$ s.t. $\Im_{Q,T} \twoheadleftarrow \Im_{Q,T\cup\{at\}}$ is not an isomorphism.

input : minimally adequate teacher of the target language $\mathcal{L}$
output: $\mathsf{Min}(\mathcal{L})$

1 $Q := T := \{\varepsilon\}$
2 **repeat**
3   **while** (Q, T) *is not* $\mathcal{L}$*-automatable* **do**
4   **if** $\varepsilon_{min} \notin \mathcal{E}$ **then**
5   add $qa \in QA$ s.t. $\Im_{Q,T}(\mathcal{L}) \rightarrowtail \Im_{Q\cup\{qa\},T}(\mathcal{L})$ is not an isomorphism to Q
6   **end**
7   **if** $\varepsilon_{min} \notin \mathcal{M}$ **then**
8   add $at \in AT$ s.t. $\Im_{Q,T}(\mathcal{L}) \twoheadleftarrow \Im_{Q,T\cup\{at\}}(\mathcal{L})$ is not an isomorphism to T
9   **end**
10   **end**
11   ask an equivalence query for the hypothesis automaton $\mathcal{H}(Q,T)$
12   **if** *the answer is no* **then**
13   add the provided counterexample and all its prefixes to Q
14   **end**
15 **until** *the answer is yes*;
16 **return** $\mathcal{H}(Q,T)$

Algorithm 4.3.2. The *optimized* FunL*-*algorithm*

In Proposition 4.2.12, the termination of the while cycle has been proved as a consequence of the finiteness of the chain of arrows not being isomorphisms among the factorizations $\Im_{Q,T}$ of the different couples.

Therefore, concerning the correctness of the optimized algorithm, the only fact to check is that such a $qa \in QA$ if $\varepsilon_{min} \notin \mathcal{E}$ and such an $at \in AT$ if $\varepsilon_{min} \notin \mathcal{M}$ exist.

Let's prove it in the following two lemmas, one being the dual of the other.

Lemma 4.3.3. *Let $\varepsilon_{min} \notin \mathcal{M}$. There exists a word $at \in AT$ such that $\Im_{Q,T} \twoheadleftarrow \Im_{Q,T\cup\{at\}}$ is not an isomorphism.*

Proof. In Lemma 4.2.9, it has been proved that $e \in \mathcal{E} \setminus \mathcal{M}$, e being obtained as follows.

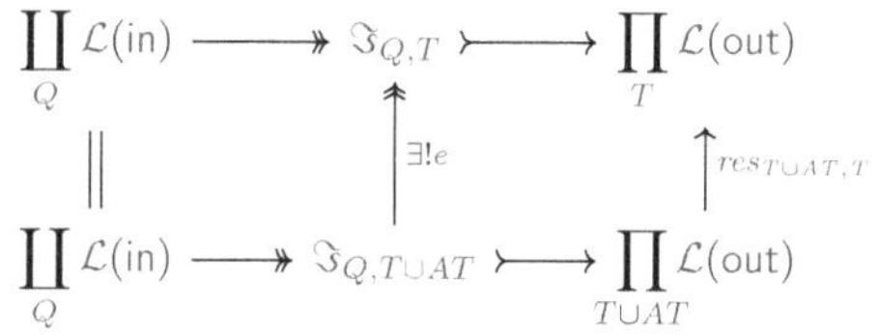

By contradiction, let's suppose that such a word at does not exist. As a consequence, one has the following situation for all $at \in AT$.

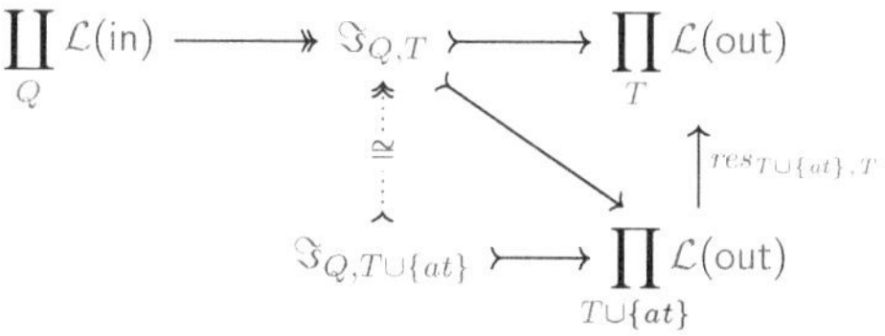

Using the diagonal arrows in the previous diagram, which are all equal when restricted to $\prod_T \mathcal{L}(\mathsf{out})$, one may obtain an arrow from $\Im_{Q,T}$ to the bigger product that makes the following diagram commute.

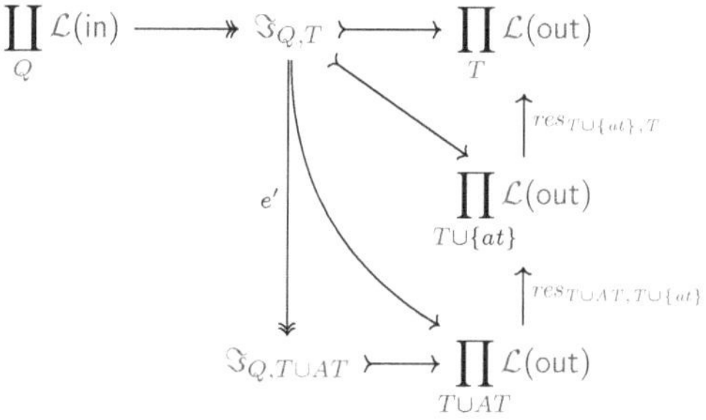

Consider the $(\mathcal{E}, \mathcal{M})$-factorization of this map, with e' denoting the arrow in $\mathcal{E}$. It is easy to see that e' is an inverse of e, as their composition is uniquely determined by the universal property of the factorization system.

This is a contradiction, as e is not an isomorphism. □

Lemma 4.3.4. *Let $\varepsilon_{min} \notin \mathcal{E}$. There exists a word $qa \in QA$ such that $\Im_{Q,T} \rightarrowtail \Im_{Q\cup\{qa\},T}$ is not an isomorphism.*

Proof. In Lemma 4.2.9, it has been proved that $m \in \mathcal{M} \setminus \mathcal{E}$, m being obtained as follows.

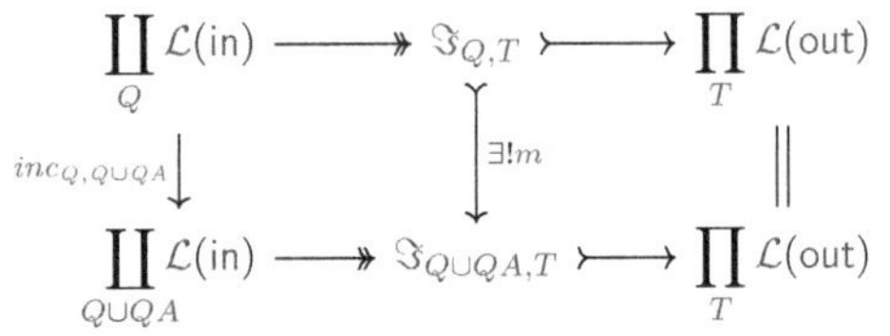

By contradiction, let's suppose that such a word does not exist. As a consequence, one has the following situation for all $qa \in QA$.

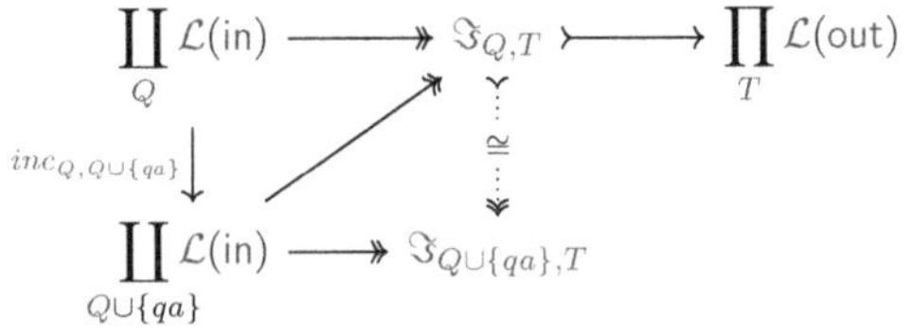

There is all is needed to build up another arrow starting from the bigger coproduct and making the following commute, with m' denoting the morphism in $\mathcal{M}$ of the $(\mathcal{E}, \mathcal{M})$-factorization of such an arrow.

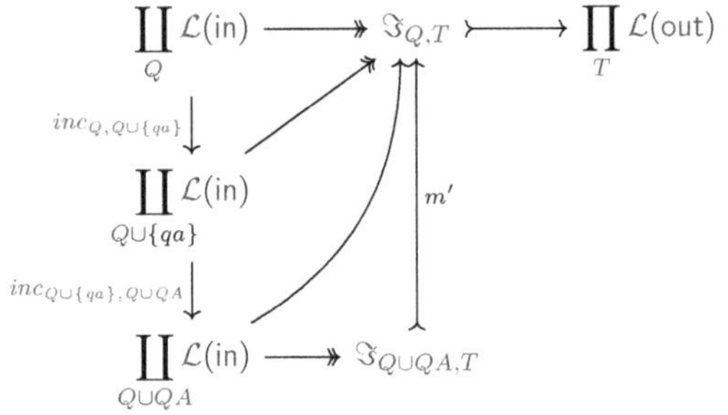

It is easy to see that m' is an inverse of m, as their composition is uniquely determined by the universal property of the factorization system.

This is a contradiction, as m is not an isomorphism. □

Proof of Theorem 4.3.1. It follows from the two lemmas above and the results about the termination and correctness of the original FunL*-algorithm. □

Chapter 5

Learning subsequential transducers categorically

In Chapter 4, it has been shown implicitly how the running instantiation of the FunL*-algorithm in the DFA case corresponds to the L^*-algorithm described in Section 1.4 (see Example 4.1.7 for details); in the same way, it may be shown that, significantly, the running instantiation of the optimized FunL*-algorithm in the SST case corresponds to the f^*-algorithm described in Section 2.5: that is the aim of this last chapter.

In order to be able to work with the more complex subsequential transducers from a categorical viewpoint, new sophisticated categories and factorization systems need to be introduced: this is done in Section 5.1; in Section 5.2, the initial and final SST are described; in Section 5.3, the notions of minimality and noetherianity in the case of SST are discussed ; finally, in Section 5.4 the optimized FunL*-algorithm is instantiated for learning SST, turning out to be the f^*-algorithm.

5.1 A category for subsequential transducers

Roughly, a subsequential transducer [7] is a deterministic finite automaton which, at each step, while reading an input letter from A, either has no transition or has a unique transition which changes deterministically the state and outputs a word from the fixed output alphabet B^*. From a categorical viewpoint, in this thesis subsequential transducers are defined as $(\mathsf{Kl}(\mathcal{T}), 1, 1)$-automata [10, 11], for a definition of $\mathsf{Kl}(\mathcal{T})$ that is now precised.

Definition 5.1.1. Let $\mathcal{T}$ be the monad defined by $\mathcal{T}X = B^* \times X + 1$: $\mathsf{Kl}(\mathcal{T})$ denotes the Kleisli category for $\mathcal{T}$.

Concretely, the objects of $\mathsf{Kl}(\mathcal{T})$ are sets, while its morphisms, denoted by negated arrows, are of the form $f\colon X \nrightarrow Y$ for a function $f\colon X \to \mathcal{T}Y$, that is, a partial function from X to $B^* \times Y$. $\bot$ now denotes the element of the singleton 1 and one may think of it as the undefined element. Given $f\colon X \nrightarrow Y$ and $g\colon Y \nrightarrow Z$, their composite $g \circ f\colon X \nrightarrow Z$ is defined on $x \in X$ by (uv, z), when $f(x) = (u, y) \in B^* \times Y$ and $g(y) = (v, z) \in B^* \times Z$ (with uv denoting the concatenation of u and v in B^*) and $f(x) = \bot$ in all other cases.

Remark 5.1.2. $(\mathsf{Kl}(\mathcal{T}), 1, 1)$-automata are equivalent to subsequential transducers in the sense of Choffrut's definition [7]: indeed, a functor $\mathcal{A}\colon \mathcal{I}_{A^*} \to \mathsf{Kl}(\mathcal{T})$ with $\mathcal{A}(\mathsf{in}) = 1$ and $\mathcal{A}(\mathsf{out}) = 1$ may be seen as a subsequential transducer by interpreting

- $\mathcal{A}(\mathsf{st})$ as the set of states,
- $\mathcal{A}(\triangleright)\colon 1 \nrightarrow \mathcal{A}(\mathsf{st})$ as either choosing an initial state together with an initial output in B^* or having an undefined initial state,
- $\mathcal{A}(a)\colon \mathcal{A}(\mathsf{st}) \nrightarrow \mathcal{A}(\mathsf{st})$ as the transition map for the letter a which associates to a given state either undefined or a pair consisting of an output word in B^* and a successor state,
- $\mathcal{A}(\triangleleft)\colon \mathcal{A}(\mathsf{st}) \nrightarrow 1$ as the final map which associates to a state either its output in B^* or undefined when it is non-accepting.

Remark 5.1.3. A transduction, i.e. a partial map from A^* to B^*, can be identified in an obvious manner with a map from A^* to arrows of the form $1 \nrightarrow 1$: this is the relation between a language in the categorical sense $\mathcal{L}\colon \mathcal{O}_{A^*} \to \mathsf{Kl}(\mathcal{T})$ and its associated transduction.

Remark 5.1.4. In $\mathsf{Kl}(\mathcal{T})$, the factorization system does not follow from general arguments: let's define now the factorization system $(\mathcal{E}_{\mathsf{Kl}(\mathcal{T})}, \mathcal{M}_{\mathsf{Kl}(\mathcal{T})})$ for $\mathsf{Kl}(\mathcal{T})$.

Given a morphism $f\colon X \nrightarrow Y$ in $\mathsf{Kl}(\mathcal{T})$, let $\pi_1(f)\colon X \to B^* + \{\bot\}$ and $\pi_2(f)\colon X \to Y + \{\bot\}$ denote the projections: if $f(x) = \bot$, then $\pi_1(f)(x) = \pi_2(f)(x) = \bot$, otherwise $f(x) = (\pi_1(f)(x), \pi_2(f)(x))$.

The class $\mathcal{E}_{\mathsf{Kl}(\mathcal{T})}$ consists of all the morphisms of the form $e\colon X \nrightarrow Y$ such that $\pi_2(e)$ is surjective (i.e. for every $y \in Y$ there exists $x \in X$ so that $\pi_2(e)(x) = y$) and the class $\mathcal{M}_{\mathsf{Kl}(\mathcal{T})}$ consists of all the morphisms of the form $m\colon X \nrightarrow Y$ such that $\pi_2(m)$ is totally defined and injective and $\pi_1(m)$ is the constant function mapping every $x \in X$ to ε.

By [11, Lemma 4.8], $(\mathcal{E}_{\mathsf{Kl}(\mathcal{T})}, \mathcal{M}_{\mathsf{Kl}(\mathcal{T})})$ is a factorization system.

5.2 Initial and final subsequential transducers

Let's compute the initial and final subsequential transducers in the category of $(\mathsf{Kl}(\mathcal{T}), 1, 1)$-automata, by making use of Lemmas 3.3.5 and 3.3.7.

Since $\mathsf{Kl}(\mathcal{T})$ has all copowers and it is easily provable that the copower of A^*-many copies of 1 in $\mathsf{Kl}(\mathcal{T})$ is A^* itself as in Set, the initial automaton for a given language can be computed as follows.

$$1 \xrightarrow{(\varepsilon,\varepsilon)} A^* \xrightarrow{\mathcal{L}?} 1 \qquad \text{(loop on } A^*\text{: } w \mapsto (\varepsilon, wa))$$

For a language $\mathcal{L}\colon \mathcal{O}_{A^*} \to \mathsf{Kl}(\mathcal{T})$, the initial subsequential transducer accepting $\mathcal{L}$ is as depicted in the diagram above. Its state space is A^*, the initial state is $\varepsilon \in A^*$ with initial output $\varepsilon \in B^*$. For an input letter $a \in A$, the corresponding transition maps w to wa and produces output $\varepsilon \in B^*$. Finally, the map $\mathcal{L}?$, which is in fact a function from A^* to $B^* + 1$, associates to a word w the value of the language at w, that is, the value computed by $\mathcal{L}(\triangleright w \triangleleft)$.

Now let's illustrate what happens for the final one.

$$1 \xrightarrow{(\mathsf{lcp}(f),\mathsf{red}(f))} \mathsf{Irr}(A^*, B^*) \xrightarrow{K \mapsto K(\varepsilon)} 1 \qquad \text{(loop on } \mathsf{Irr}(A^*,B^*)\text{: } K \mapsto (\mathsf{lcp}(K(a-)), \mathsf{red}(K(a-))))$$

Somewhat surprisingly, $\mathsf{Kl}(\mathcal{T})$-automata also fit in the scope of Lemma 3.3.7, as it will be proved that the object $\mathsf{Irr}(A^*, B^*)$ introduced in Definition 5.2.1 is the power of A^*-many copies of 1 in $\mathsf{Kl}(\mathcal{T})$.

First, let's recall some definitions already given in Chapter 2:

- given a transduction K, $\mathsf{lcp}(K)$ is undefined if K is nowhere defined, and the longest common prefix of the words in $\{K(u) \mid u \in A^*\}$ otherwise (Definition 2.2.21);
- a transduction K is irreducible if $\mathsf{lcp}(K) = \varepsilon$ (Definition 2.2.22);
- for all K not nowhere defined, $\mathsf{red}(K)$ is the only irreducible transduction such that $K(u) = \mathsf{lcp}(K)\mathsf{red}(K)(u)$, i.e. the transduction in which the prefix $\mathsf{lcp}(K)$ has been stripped away from all outputs, while if K is nowhere defined, $\mathsf{red}(K)$ is nowhere defined too (Definition 2.2.23).

Definition 5.2.1. $\mathsf{Irr}(A^*, B^*)$ denotes the set of irreducible transductions from A^* to B^*.

Lemma 5.2.2. *$\mathsf{Irr}(A^*, B^*)$ is the product of A^*-many copies of 1 in $\mathsf{Kl}(\mathcal{T})$.*

Proof. Let's check the universal property of the product, so let's suppose there are:

- an object X in the category $\mathsf{Kl}(\mathcal{T})$;
- a family of arrows $\{h_w\}_{w \in A^*}$ such that $h_w\colon X \nrightarrow 1$.

The proof consists in showing that there exists a unique morphism h such that the following diagram commutes:

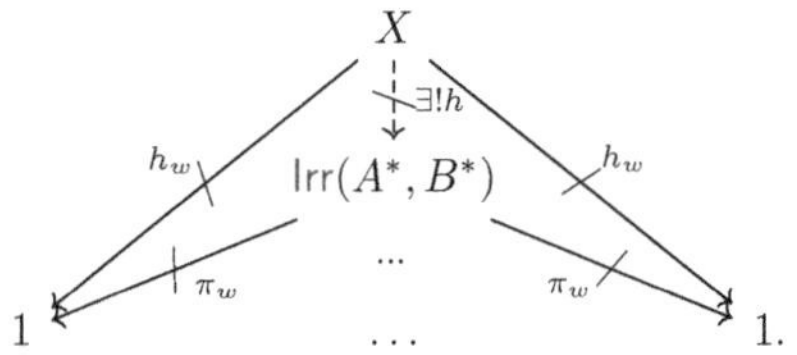

Note that the arrows π_w denoting the projections of the product are defined as follows, for all $w \in A^*$:

$$\pi_w \colon \mathsf{Irr}(A^*, B^*) \nrightarrow 1$$
$$K \mapsto K(w).$$

Concerning the existence, first let's define a transduction K_x for all $x \in X$:

$$K_x \colon A^* \rightharpoonup B^*$$
$$w \mapsto h_w(x);$$

then, let's define h as follows:

$$h \colon X \nrightarrow \mathsf{Irr}(A^*, B^*)$$
$$x \mapsto (\mathsf{lcp}(K_x), \mathsf{red}(K_x)).$$

Obviously, $h(x)$ is undefined if and only if the transduction K_x is nowhere defined.

h satisfies the required properties: in fact, $(\pi_w \circ h)(x) = \pi_w(\mathsf{lcp}(K_x), \mathsf{red}(K_x)) = \mathsf{lcp}(K_x)(\mathsf{red}(K_x)(w)) = \mathsf{lcp}(K_x)\mathsf{lcp}(K_x)^{-1}K_x(w) = K_x(w) = h_w(x)$, for all $x \in X$ and for all $w \in A^*$.

Concerning the uniqueness, let's suppose there exists a morphism h' satisfying the required properties and let's show that $h' = h$; recall that, using the factorization system introduced in Remark 5.1.4, $h' = h$ if and only if $\pi_1(h') = \pi_1(h)$ and $\pi_2(h') = \pi_2(h)$, that is, they are equal in each component.

Notice the difference in notation: π_1 and π_2 denote the projections of the factorization system, whereas π_w is used to denote the projections of the product.

By virtue of the universal property, one has that $\pi_1(h)(x)\pi_w(\pi_2(h)(x)) = (\pi_w \circ h)(x) = (\pi_w \circ h')(x) = \pi_1(h')(x)\pi_w(\pi_2(h')(x))$ for all $x \in X$ and for all $w \in A^*$, so:

$$\pi_1(h)(x)\pi_2(h)(x)(w) = \pi_1(h')(x)\pi_2(h')(x)(w) \ \forall x \in X \ \forall w \in A^*. \tag{5.2.3}$$

Now let's fix arbitrarily $x \in X$: it is clear that $h(x)$ is undefined if and only if $h'(x)$ is, so let's suppose that $h(x)$ is defined, as well as $h'(x)$.

First, as $\pi_2(h)(x) \in \mathsf{Irr}(A^*, B^*)$, there exist $w_1, w_2 \in A^*$ such that $\mathsf{lcp}(\{\pi_2(h)(x)(w_1), \pi_2(h)(x)(w_2)\}) = \varepsilon$; analogously, as $\pi_2(h')(x) \in \mathsf{Irr}(A^*, B^*)$, there exist $w_3, w_4 \in A^*$ such that $\mathsf{lcp}(\{\pi_2(h')(x)(w_3), \pi_2(h')(x)(w_4)\}) = \varepsilon$.

By (5.2.3):

$$\pi_1(h)(x)\pi_2(h)(x)(w_i) = \pi_1(h')(x)\pi_2(h')(x)(w_i)\ \forall i \in \{1,\dots,4\};$$

in particular, taking the longest common prefix of the two correlated sets:

$$\pi_1(h)(x)\mathsf{lcp}\left(\bigcup_{i=1,\dots,4} \pi_2(h)(x)(w_i)\right) = \pi_1(h')(x)\mathsf{lcp}\left(\bigcup_{i=1,\dots,4} \pi_2(h')(x)(w_i)\right),$$

$$\pi_1(h)(x) = \pi_1(h')(x);$$

hence, as $x \in X$ is arbitrary:

$$\pi_1(h) = \pi_1(h'). \tag{5.2.4}$$

Secondly, by (5.2.3) and (5.2.4):

$$\pi_2(h)(x)(w) = \pi_2(h')(x)(w)\ \forall x \in X\ \forall w \in A^*,$$

$$\pi_2(h)(x) = \pi_2(h')(x)\ \forall x \in X,$$

$$\pi_2(h) = \pi_2(h'). \tag{5.2.5}$$

This concludes the proof. □

So let's come back to the final subsequential transducer for a given language $\mathcal{L}\colon \mathcal{O}_{A^*} \to \mathsf{Kl}(\mathcal{T})$, f being its associated transduction (see Remark 5.1.3).

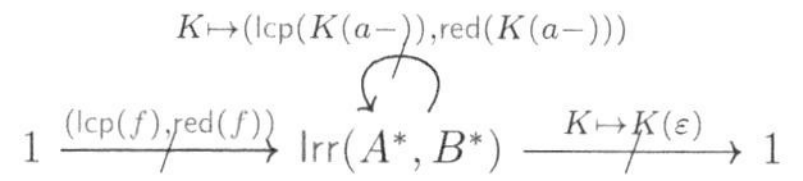

The final automaton for the language $\mathcal{L}$, as depicted in the diagram immediately above, can now be described as an automaton that has irreducible transductions as states. The initial map is the constant map equal to $(\mathsf{lcp}(f), \mathsf{red}(f))$ (or undefined if f is nowhere defined). When reading the letter a from state K, the automaton jumps to $\mathsf{red}(K(a-))$, in which $K(a-)$ is such that $K(a-)(u) = K(au)$ (or undefined if $K(a-)$ is nowhere defined). The final map sends an irreducible transduction K to $K(\varepsilon)$.

5.3 Minimality and noetherianity for SST

In order to find out the minimal automaton in the category of $(\mathsf{Kl}(\mathcal{T}), 1, 1)$-automata, let's see how Theorem 3.3.9 instantiates in the case of subsequential transducers for a given language $\mathcal{L}\colon \mathcal{O}_{A^*} \to \mathsf{Kl}(\mathcal{T})$.

Recall that such a functor may be interpreted as a transduction f from A^* to B^* (see Remark 5.1.3).

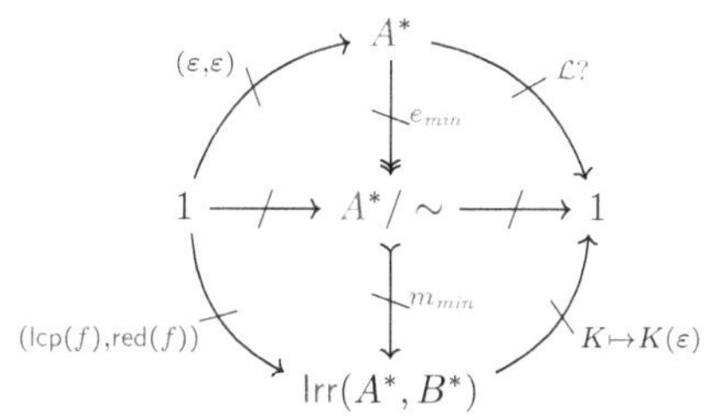

The only arrow from A^* to $\mathsf{Irr}(A^*, B^*)$ making the diagram commute maps an element $w \in A^*$ to the couple $(\mathsf{lcp}(f(w-)), \mathsf{red}(f(w-)))$, where $f(w-)(v) = f(wv)$ for all $v \in A^*$; the factorization of such an arrow:

- first maps an element $w \in A^*$ to the couple $(\mathsf{lcp}(f(w-)), [w])$ $[w]$ being its equivalence class according to the syntactic equivalence relation over f defined in Section 2.3;

- secondly maps an equivalence class $[w]$ to the couple $(\varepsilon, \mathsf{red}(f(w-)))$.

The minimal subsequential transducer accepting $\mathcal{L}$ is depicted below in detail.

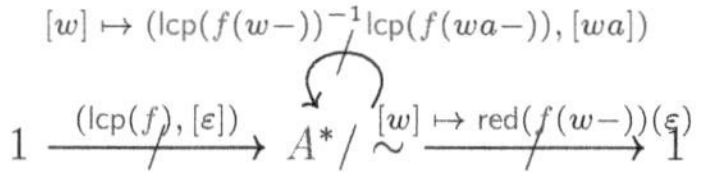

As one can see, the automaton turns out to be the minimal SST described in Proposition 2.3.12, as long as the transduction to learn is subsequential, that is, the index of the syntactic equivalence relation over f, corresponding to the cardinality of the set of states, is finite.

What is the relation between the finiteness of the set of states and the condition of its noetherianity requested for the FunL*-algorithm to work? In $\mathsf{Kl}(\mathcal{T})$, they mean the same thing.

Lemma 5.3.1. *An object X of $\mathsf{Kl}(\mathcal{T})$ is $(\mathcal{E}_{\mathsf{Kl}(\mathcal{T})}, \mathcal{M}_{\mathsf{Kl}(\mathcal{T})})$-noetherian if and only if it is finite.*

Proof. First of all, let's recall that an isomorphism in $\mathsf{Kl}(\mathcal{T})$ is an arrow $f\colon X \twoheadrightarrow Y$ such that $\pi_1(f)$ is the constant function equal to ε and $\pi_2(f)$ is a bijection.

Let's assume that X is finite and show that it is $(\mathcal{E}_{\mathsf{Kl}(\mathcal{T})}, \mathcal{M}_{\mathsf{Kl}(\mathcal{T})})$-noetherian. For this, consider two commutative diagrams as follows:

Concerning the left diagram, recall first that for all $e\colon Y \twoheadrightarrow Z$ from $\mathcal{E}_{\mathsf{Kl}(\mathcal{T})}$, $\pi_2(e)$ is surjective. Hence, if Y is finite, then so is Z and furthermore $|Y| \geqslant |Z|$. Applied to the diagram, one obtains that $(|Y_i|)_i$ is a non-decreasing sequence of non-negative integers bounded by $|X|$. Hence, for all sufficiently large i (say, larger than i_0), $|Y_i| = |Y_{i+1}|$ and as a consequence $\pi_2(e_i)$ is a totally defined bijection.

Given an arrow $f\colon Y \twoheadrightarrow Z$, denote by $||f||$ the sum of the $|\pi_1(f)(y)|$ for $y \in Y$ (the sum of the sizes of all output words). Consider now some $g\colon Z \twoheadrightarrow T$. It is easy to see that if $\pi_2(f)$ is surjective and $\pi_2(g)$ is totally defined, then $||g \circ f|| \geqslant ||g|| + ||f||$. It follows that $||f_i|| \geqslant ||f_{i+1}|| + ||e_i||$ for all $i \geqslant i_0$. Since $||f_{i_0}||$ is finite, it follows that $||e_i|| = 0$ for all sufficiently large i. Hence, e_i is an isomorphism: the first item of Definition 4.2.3 has been established.

Concerning the right diagram, note that for all $m\colon Y \rightarrowtail Z$ from $\mathcal{M}_{\mathsf{Kl}(\mathcal{T})}$, $\pi_2(m)$ is totally defined and injective. Hence, if Z is finite, Y also is and $|Y| \leqslant |Z|$. It follows that $(|Z_i|)_i$ is a non decreasing sequence, bounded by $|X|$. Hence, for all sufficiently large i, $|Z_i| = |Z_{i+1}|$. It follows that $\pi_2(m_i)$ is an injection from Z_i to Z_{i+1} with $|Z_i| = |Z_{i+1}|$ finite. Thus $\pi_2(m_i)$ is a bijection. Since furthermore $\pi_1(m_i) = \varepsilon$ by assumption, one obtains that m_i is an isomorphism: the second item of Definition 4.2.3 has been established.

Overall, X is $(\mathcal{E}_{\mathsf{Kl}(\mathcal{T})}, \mathcal{M}_{\mathsf{Kl}(\mathcal{T})})$-noetherian.

For the converse implication, let's consider a $(\mathcal{E}_{\mathsf{Kl}(\mathcal{T})}, \mathcal{M}_{\mathsf{Kl}(\mathcal{T})})$-noetherian set X to show that it is finite. For the sake of contradiction, assume it is infinite, and let $Z_0 \subsetneq Z_1 \subsetneq Z_2 \subsetneq \cdots$ be a sequence of subsets of Z. Let now $m_i \colon Z_i \not\rightarrowtail Z_{i+1}$ be the inclusion from Z_i into Z_{i+1}, and $f_i \colon Z_i \not\rightarrowtail X$ be the inclusion of Z_i into X. These arrows show that the second item of 4.2.3 does not hold. □

5.4 The learning algorithm for SST from the categorical algorithm

Let's see how the optimized FunL*-algorithm instantiates to the case of subsequential transducers.

input : minimally adequate teacher of the target language $\mathcal{L}$
output: $\mathsf{Min}(\mathcal{L})$
$Q := T := \{\varepsilon\}$
repeat
  while *(Q, T) is not $\mathcal{L}$-automatable* **do**
    if $\varepsilon_{min} \notin \mathcal{E}_{\mathsf{Kl}(\mathcal{T})}$ **then**
      add $qa \in QA$ s.t. $\mathfrak{I}_{Q,T}(\mathcal{L}) \not\rightarrowtail \mathfrak{I}_{Q \cup \{qa\},T}(\mathcal{L})$ is not an isomorphism to Q
    end
    if $\varepsilon_{min} \notin \mathcal{M}_{\mathsf{Kl}(\mathcal{T})}$ **then**
      add $at \in AT$ s.t. $\mathfrak{I}_{Q,T}(\mathcal{L}) \not\twoheadleftarrow \mathfrak{I}_{Q,T \cup \{at\}}(\mathcal{L})$ is not an isomorphism to T
    end
  end
  ask an equivalence query for the hypothesis automaton $\mathcal{H}(Q, T)$
  if *the answer is no* **then**
    add the provided counterexample and all its prefixes to Q
  end
until *the answer is yes*;
return $\mathcal{H}(Q, T)$

Algorithm 5.4.1. The optimized FunL*-algorithm to instantiate.

In this case, the target language $\mathcal{L}$ is assumed to be a $(\mathsf{Kl}(\mathcal{T}), 1, 1)$-language and the learner wants to learn the minimal subsequential transducer accepting $\mathcal{L}$.

Thinking of the language to learn as a transduction $f \colon A^* \rightharpoonup B^*$, let's recall the T-syntactic equivalence relation over f: for all $q_1, q_2 \in Q$, $q_1 \sim_T q_2$ if and only if the related reductions are equal, i.e. $\mathsf{red}(f(q_1-)|_T) = \mathsf{red}(f(q_2-)|_T)$, $f(q-)|_T$ being the restriction of $f(q-)$ to T.

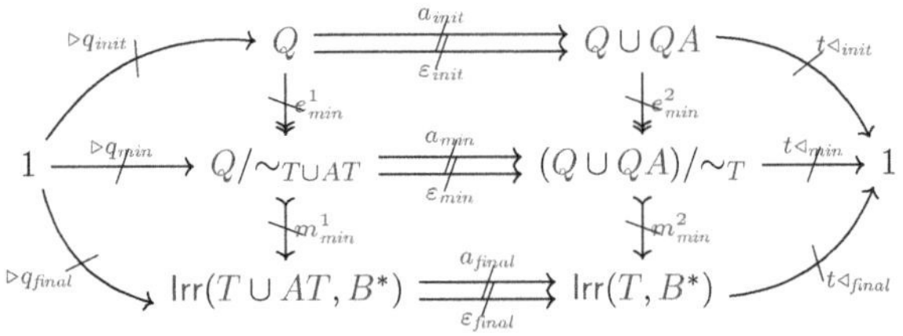

The aim is to relate the FunL*-algorithm to the specific properties of the couple (Q,T) already described in the presentation of the f^*-algorithm:

- f-completeness (Definition 2.4.1),

$$\forall q \in Q \; \forall a \in A \; \exists \tilde{q} \in Q \colon \tilde{q} \sim_T qa; \tag{5.4.2}$$

- f-correctness (Definition 2.4.2),

$$\forall q_1, q_2 \in Q \; \forall a \in A \; \forall t \in T \; (q_1 \sim_T q_2 \Rightarrow q_1 \sim_{T\cup\{at\}} q_2); \tag{5.4.3}$$

- f-consistency (Definition 2.4.3),

$$\forall q \in Q \; \forall a \in A \; \mathsf{lcp}(f(q-)|_T) \sqsubseteq \mathsf{lcp}(f(qa-)|_T). \tag{5.4.4}$$

First of all, let's check when a certain couple (Q,T) is $\mathcal{L}$-automatable, that is, when the arrow ε_{min} in $\mathsf{Auto}(\mathcal{L}_{Q,T})$ is an isomorphism.

In the diagram, ε_{min} turns out to be the map $Q/{\sim_{T\cup AT}} \nrightarrow (Q \cup QA)/{\sim_T}$, $[q]_{T\cup AT} \mapsto (\mathsf{lcp}(f(q-)|_{T\cup AT})^{-1}\mathsf{lcp}(f(q-)|_T), [q]_T)$, the first set of states being Q quotiented by $\sim_{T\cup AT}$, the second set of states being the quotient of $Q \cup QA$ by $\sim_T$.

Notice that ε_{min} is an isomorphism if and only if $\varepsilon_{min} \in \mathcal{E}_{\mathsf{Kl}(\mathcal{T})}$ and $\varepsilon_{min} \in \mathcal{M}_{\mathsf{Kl}(\mathcal{T})}$, so let's see separately what these two conditions mean:

$$\begin{aligned} \varepsilon_{min} \in \mathcal{E}_{\mathsf{Kl}(\mathcal{T})} &\Leftrightarrow \pi_2(\varepsilon_{min}) \text{ is surjective} \\ &\Leftrightarrow \forall q \in Q \; \forall a \in A \; \exists \tilde{q} \in Q \text{ s.t. } \tilde{q} \sim_T qa \\ &\Leftrightarrow (Q,T) \text{ is } f\text{-complete;} \end{aligned}$$

$$\begin{aligned} \varepsilon_{min} \in \mathcal{M}_{\mathsf{Kl}(\mathcal{T})} &\Leftrightarrow \pi_2(\varepsilon_{min}) \text{ is injective and } \pi_1(\varepsilon_{min}) \text{ is constantly equal to } \varepsilon \\ &\Leftrightarrow \forall q, q' \in Q \; (q \sim_T q' \Rightarrow q \sim_{T\cup AT} q') \text{ and} \\ &\qquad \forall q \in Q \; \mathsf{lcp}(f(q-)|_{T\cup AT}) = \mathsf{lcp}(f(q-)|_T) \\ &\Leftrightarrow (Q,T) \text{ is } f\text{-correct and } f\text{-consistent.} \end{aligned}$$

A full proof should be given for the last equivalence: to do that, it behoves the author to provide a simple remark.

Remark 5.4.5. It is easy to see that the property of f-consistency (5.4.4) is equivalent to the aforementioned fact that for all $q \in Q$ $\mathsf{lcp}(f(q-)|_{T\cup AT}) = \mathsf{lcp}(f(q-)|_T)$, so the two may be used indistinctly.

Lemma 5.4.6. *Assume the couple (Q,T) is f-consistent. Such a couple is f-correct if and only if for all $q, q' \in Q$ $q \sim_T q'$ implies that $q \sim_{T\cup AT} q'$.*

Proof. Suppose that the f-consistent couple (Q,T) is f-correct and suppose that $q \sim_T q'$ too, with $q, q' \in Q$.

By means of the f-correctness, one knows that $q \sim_{T\cup\{at\}} q'$ for all $at \in AT$, that is, $\mathsf{lcp}(f(q-)|_{T\cup\{at\}})^{-1}f(qt') = \mathsf{lcp}(f(q'-)|_{T\cup\{at\}})^{-1}f(q't')$ for all $t' \in T\cup\{at\}$; thanks to the f-consistency, $\mathsf{lcp}(f(q-)|_{T\cup\{at\}}) = \mathsf{lcp}(f(q-)|_T) = \mathsf{lcp}(f(q-)|_{T\cup AT})$ and $\mathsf{lcp}(f(q'-)|_{T\cup\{at\}}) = \mathsf{lcp}(f(q'-)|_T) = \mathsf{lcp}(f(q'-)|_{T\cup AT})$: hence,

$$\mathsf{lcp}(f(q-)|_{T\cup AT})^{-1}f(qt') = \mathsf{lcp}(f(q'-)|_{T\cup AT})^{-1}f(q't')\ \forall t' \in T\cup AT,$$

that is, $q \sim_{T\cup AT} q'$.

For the converse implication, let's suppose that $q_1 \sim_T q_2$; by hypothesis, $q_1 \sim_{T\cup AT} q_2$, so $\mathsf{lcp}(f(q_1-)|_{T\cup AT})^{-1}f(q_1t') = \mathsf{lcp}(f(q_2-)|_{T\cup AT})^{-1}f(q_2t')$ for all $t' \in T\cup AT$; thanks to the f-consistency, the equality

$$\mathsf{lcp}(f(q_1-)|_{T\cup\{at\}})^{-1}f(q_1t') = \mathsf{lcp}(f(q_2'-)|_{T\cup\{at\}})^{-1}f(q_2t')\ \forall t' \in T\cup\{at\}$$

also holds for all $a \in A$ and for all $t \in T$: this is exactly the condition of f-correctness.

This concludes the proof. □

In particular, it has been proven that a couple (Q,T) is $\mathcal{L}$-automatable if and only if it is f-complete, f-correct and f-consistent.

What remains to do is to instantiate lines 5 and 8 of the optimized FunL*-algorithm.

First of all, let's apply Lemma 4.2.8 in order to find the canonical morphisms out:

- $\Im_{Q,T}(\mathcal{L}) \not\mapsto \Im_{Q\cup\{qa\},T}(\mathcal{L})$ turns out to be the map $Q/{\sim_T} \not\mapsto (Q\cup\{qa\})/{\sim_T}, [q]_T \mapsto (\varepsilon, [q]_T)$;
- $\Im_{Q,T}(\mathcal{L}) \not\leftarrow \Im_{Q,T\cup\{at\}}(\mathcal{L})$ turns out to be the map $Q/{\sim_T} \not\leftarrow Q/{\sim_{T\cup\{at\}}}, [q]_{T\cup\{at\}} \mapsto (\mathsf{lcp}(f(q-)|_{T\cup\{at\}})^{-1}\mathsf{lcp}(f(q-)|_T), [q]_T)$.

Now it is possible to translate lines 5 and 8 as follows:

$$\begin{aligned}
\text{line } 5 &= \text{add } qa \in QA \text{ s.t. } \Im_{Q,T}(\mathcal{L}) \not\mapsto \Im_{Q\cup\{qa\},T}(\mathcal{L}) \\
&\quad \text{is not an isomorphism to } Q \\
&\Leftrightarrow \text{add } qa \in QA \text{ s.t } Q/{\sim_T} \not\mapsto (Q\cup\{qa\})/{\sim_T}, [q]_T \mapsto (\varepsilon, [q]_T) \\
&\quad \text{is not an isomorphism to } Q \\
&\Leftrightarrow \text{add } qa \in QA \text{ s.t. } \nexists \widetilde{q} \in Q\colon \widetilde{q} \sim_T qa \text{ to } Q;
\end{aligned}$$

$$\begin{aligned}
\text{line } 8 &= \text{add } at \in AT \text{ s.t. } \Im_{Q,T}(\mathcal{L}) \not\leftarrow \Im_{Q,T\cup\{at\}}(\mathcal{L}) \\
&\quad \text{is not an isomorphism to } T \\
&\Leftrightarrow \text{add } at \in AT \text{ s.t. } Q/{\sim_T} \not\leftarrow Q/{\sim_{T\cup\{at\}}}, \\
&\quad [q]_{T\cup\{at\}} \mapsto (\mathsf{lcp}(f(q-)|_{T\cup\{at\}})^{-1}\mathsf{lcp}(f(q-)|_T), [q]_T) \\
&\quad \text{is not an isomorphism to } T \\
&\Leftrightarrow \text{add } at \in AT \text{ s.t. } \exists q_1, q_2 \in Q\colon q_1 \sim_T q_2 \wedge q_1 \nsim_{T\cup\{at\}} q_2 \text{ to } T, \text{ or} \\
&\quad \text{add } at \in AT \text{ s.t. } \exists q \in Q\colon \mathsf{lcp}(f(q-)|_T) \neq \mathsf{lcp}(f(q-)|_{T\cup\{at\}}) \text{ to } T.
\end{aligned}$$

The objective of this chapter has been achieved: the instantiated optimized FunL*-algorithm in the SST case turns out to be the f^*-algorithm for learning subsequential transducers presented in Chapter 2.

input : minimally adequate teacher of the subsequential target transduction f
output: minimal SST accepting f

$Q := T := \{\varepsilon\}$
repeat
  while *(Q, T) is not f-complete, f-correct and f-consistent* **do**
    if *(Q, T) is not f-complete* **then**
      add $qa \in QA$ s.t. $\nexists \tilde{q} \in Q\colon \tilde{q} \sim_T qa$ to Q
    end
    if *(Q, T) is not f-correct* **then**
      add $at \in AT$ s.t. $\exists q_1, q_2 \in Q\colon q_1 \sim_T q_2 \wedge q_1 \nsim_{T \cup \{at\}} q_2$ to T
    end
    if *(Q, T) is not f-consistent* **then**
      add $at \in AT$ s.t. $\exists q \in Q\colon \mathsf{lcp}(f(q-)|_T) \neq \mathsf{lcp}(f(q-)|_{T \cup \{at\}})$ to T
    end
  end
  ask an equivalence query for the hypothesis SST associated to the couple (Q, T)
  if *the answer is no* **then**
    add the provided counterexample and all its prefixes to Q
  end
until *the answer is yes*;
return *the hypothesis SST associated to the couple (Q, T)*

Algorithm 5.4.7. The instantiated optimized FunL*-algorithm, aka the f^*-algorithm.

Conclusion

In this thesis, an original categorical version of Angluin's L^*-algorithm for learning word automata was described: the focus was on providing a minimalistic category theoretic framework for learning, with as few assumptions as possible, emphasizing along the way the deep connection between learning and minimization.

The author let the reader deal with both approaches:

- the technical and specialized approach based on query learning in Part I, by which Vilar extended Angluin's algorithm for learning deterministic finite automata to subsequential transducers, exploiting the specifics of such automata;
- the generic and powerful approach based on category theory in Part II, by which the author and his external supervisors came to a new algorithm instantiable to deterministic finite automata, subsequential transducers and possibly even other forms of word automata.

Fascinatingly enough, the new algorithm makes it possible to understand the global patterns underlying the different learning algorithms and use them in order to derivate a version of the algorithm for each automaton: that is the charm and strength of category theory.

Concerning the future work, so far the FunL*-algorithm does not cover instances of the L^*-like algorithms such as nominal automata or automata over trees: a natural continuation is to develop these generalizations.

Another aspect to understand is the complexity of this algorithm in terms of number of evaluation and equivalence queries: since the FunL*-algorithm follows the original L^*-algorithm scheme, it clearly inherits its good complexity characteristics in the known cases, but what could be investigated is how to measure this complexity in more abstract categories.

Acknowledgements

First of all, I would like to thank the external supervisors of this thesis, Professors Thomas Colcombet and Daniela Petrişan of Université de Paris, for having given me the opportunity to write the research article on which this thesis is based during a five-month Erasmus in Paris.

I thank Professor Andrea Montoli from my department as well for serving his role of internal supervisor with great care and professionalism.

I am also grateful to the fellow students who have shown interest for my work and shared their impressions with me.

Finally, I wish to express my heartfelt thanks to my family and my friends for always being an unfailing support for me.

Ringraziamenti

Prima di tutto, vorrei ringraziare i relatori esterni, i professori Thomas Colcombet e Daniela Petrişan dell'Université de Paris, per avermi dato l'opportunità di scrivere l'articolo di ricerca sul quale questa tesi è basata nel corso di un Erasmus di cinque mesi a Parigi.

Ringrazio anche il professor Andrea Montoli del mio dipartimento per aver adempiuto al suo ruolo di relatore interno con particolare attenzione e professionalità.

Sono inoltre grato ai colleghi di studi che hanno mostrato interesse per il mio lavoro e condiviso le loro impressioni con me.

Infine, desidero rivolgere un caloroso ringraziamento alla mia famiglia e ai miei amici per essermi sempre di costante supporto.

Bibliography

[1] Dana Angluin. Learning regular sets from queries and counterexamples. *Inf. Comput., 75, 87-106*, 1987.

[2] Dana Angluin, Sarah Eisenstat, and Dana Fisman. Learning regular languages via alternating automata. In *Proceedings of the Twenty-Fourth International Joint Conference on Artificial Intelligence, IJCAI 2015, Buenos Aires, Argentina, July 25-31, 2015*, pages 3308–3314, 2015.

[3] Dana Angluin and Dana Fisman. Learning regular omega languages. *Theor. Comput. Sci.*, 650:57–72, 2016.

[4] Simone Barlocco, Clemens Kupke, and Jurriaan Rot. Coalgebra learning via duality. In *FoSSaCS*, volume 11425 of *Lecture Notes in Computer Science*, pages 62–79. Springer, 2019.

[5] Benedikt Bollig, Peter Habermehl, Carsten Kern, and Martin Leucker. Angluin-style learning of NFA. In *IJCAI 2009, Proceedings of the 21st International Joint Conference on Artificial Intelligence, Pasadena, California, USA, July 11-17, 2009*, pages 1004–1009, 2009.

[6] Véronique Bruyère and Christophe Reutenauer. A proof of Choffrut's theorem on subsequential functions. *Theoretical Computer Science*, 215(1):329–335, 1999.

[7] Christian Choffrut. A generalization of Ginsburg and Rose's characterization of G-S-M mappings. In *ICALP*, volume 71 of *Lecture Notes in Computer Science*, pages 88–103. Springer, 1979.

[8] Christian Choffrut. Minimizing subsequential transducers: a survey. *Theor. Comput. Sci.*, 292:131–143, 2003.

[9] Thomas Colcombet, Daniela Petrişan, and Riccardo Stabile. Learning automata and transducers: a categorical approach. In Christel Baier and Jean Goubault-Larrecq, editors, *29th EACSL Annual Conference on Computer Science Logic (CSL 2021)*, volume 183 of *Leibniz International Proceedings in Informatics (LIPIcs)*, pages 15:1–15:17, Dagstuhl, Germany, 2021. Schloss Dagstuhl–Leibniz-Zentrum für Informatik.

[10] Thomas Colcombet and Daniela Petrişan. Automata minimization: a functorial approach. In *7th Conference on Algebra and Coalgebra in Computer Science, CALCO 2017, June 12-16, 2017, Ljubljana, Slovenia*, pages 8:1–8:16, 2017.

[11] Thomas Colcombet and Daniela Petrişan. Automata minimization: a functorial approach. *Logical Methods in Computer Science*, Volume 16, Issue 1, 2020.

[12] Samuel Drews and Loris D'Antoni. Learning symbolic automata. In *Tools and Algorithms for the Construction and Analysis of Systems - 23rd International Conference, TACAS 2017, Held as Part of the European Joint Conferences on Theory and Practice of Software, ETAPS 2017, Uppsala, Sweden, April 22-29, 2017, Proceedings, Part I*, pages 173–189, 2017.

[13] John E. Hopcroft and Jeffrey D. Ullman. *Formal languages and their relation to automata.* Addison-Wesley Series in Computer Science. Addison-Wesley Pub. Co., 1969.

[14] John E. Hopcroft and Jeffrey D. Ullman. *Introduction to automata theory, languages, and computation.* Addison-Wesley Series in Computer Science. Addison-Wesley Pub. Co., 1979.

[15] Bart Jacobs and Alexandra Silva. Automata learning: a categorical perspective. In *Horizons of the Mind*, volume 8464 of *Lecture Notes in Computer Science*, pages 384–406. Springer, 2014.

[16] Joshua Moerman, Matteo Sammartino, Alexandra Silva, Bartek Klin, and Michal Szynwelski. Learning nominal automata. In *Proceedings of the 44th ACM SIGPLAN Symposium on Principles of Programming Languages, POPL 2017, Paris, France, January 18-20, 2017*, pages 613–625, 2017.

[17] José Oncina, Pedro García, and Enrique Vidal. Learning subsequential transducers for pattern recognition interpretation task. *IEEE Transactions on Pattern Analysis and Machine Intelligence*, Volume 15, Number 5:448–458, 1993.

[18] Christophe Reutenauer. Subsequential functions: characterizations, minimization, examples. In *Proc. IMYCS '90*, volume 464 of *Lecture Notes in Computer Science*, pages 62–79. Springer, 1990.

[19] Emily Riehl. *Factorization systems.* 2008.

[20] Henning Urbat and Lutz Schröder. Automata learning: an algebraic approach. In *LICS*, pages 900–914. ACM, 2020.

[21] Gerco van Heerdt, Matteo Sammartino, and Alexandra Silva. CALF: Categorical Automata Learning Framework. In Valentin Goranko and Mads Dam, editors, *26th EACSL Annual Conference on Computer Science Logic (CSL 2017)*, volume 82 of *Leibniz International Proceedings in Informatics (LIPIcs)*, pages 29:1–29:24, Dagstuhl, Germany, 2017. Schloss Dagstuhl–Leibniz-Zentrum fuer Informatik.

[22] Juan Miguel Vilar. Query learning of subsequential transducers. In *Grammatical Inference: Learning Syntax from Sentences, 3rd International Colloquium, ICGI-96, Montpellier, France, September 25-27, 1996, Proceedings*, pages 72–83, 1996.

Milton Keynes UK
Ingram Content Group UK Ltd.
UKHW010757110624
444053UK00004B/297